MW00616922

# THE LANDSCAPE
# of GRIEF

*The Passage Through Grief to Hope*

**Marsha Barnosky, LMSW, ACSW**

Published by Dappled Light Press
53 N Third Ave, Fruitport, MI 49415
Copyright © 2022 by Marsha Barnosky, LMSW, ACSW
Library of Congress Control Number: 2022903820
ISBN: 978-1-7374026-1-9

Dappled Light Press

# Acknowledgments

The book you are holding is the culmination of years of work with people grieving a loss. To all of you, thank you for trusting and teaching me.

I would like to extend my gratitude to the following:

To my developmental co-editors: Rachael Thompson Shah, Mickey Maroon, LCSW, Laura Huggler, Ph.D., and Lori Kerlin, DBA, SPHR who provided invaluable feedback.

To Nancy Johns MS, OTR/L, whose gentle nudging helped me pick up and finish what I started years earlier.

To my copy editor, Mary Wykoff whose keen eye caught everything I didn't and kept me on task and moving forward.

To my amazing husband Carl for his loving, wise and supportive presence. Your faith in me allowed me to do what I didn't think was possible.

Finally, my love and thanks to the Holy Spirit, who led and inspired me to keep going when I was tired and discouraged. It took longer than planned but Your timing is always perfect.

## FOR DEE

Twin sets of wings blazing
My eyes wide in disbelief
Golden grace-crowned sentinels
So calm and blessing me

*Birds of a Feather*

# Preface

The most common question people ask after hearing what I do is, "Isn't that depressing?"

Nothing could be further from the truth. In fact, it is an honor to witness someone with a broken heart courageously face what our culture ignores. And when they grow through their grief to renew and reinvent themselves, I am inspired—and humbled.

My professional life has centered on helping others live with and grow through grief and loss. Looking back on my life, it should not be a surprise. From an early age, I was aware of the legacy of loss within my own extended family. My grandmother and mother both struggled with multiple deaths early in their lives; my mother, until Alzheimer's took her memories.

## My Grief History

I may not have walked in your shoes, but I have walked through my own experiences of grief and loss to a place of healing and renewal.

I have endured the deaths of my parents and my maternal grandmother, the only grandparent I ever knew. I have faced infertility, separation, divorce, and the sudden deaths of a family member and a close friend. I was unprepared for how overwhelmed and frightened I was or how alone I felt.

My professional education and experience did nothing (and does nothing) to spare my broken heart. Like anyone else, I found it hard to navigate through the mire of loss, transition, and change. However, life's twists and turns continue to inspire me to encourage others to mourn their losses so they can more fully live their lives with hope.

I have worked with individuals, families, and businesses before and after a death working in hospice care and private practice. This work informed my perspective on death and grief and my perspective on life as well.

I believe we are here to care for one another. At some point in our lives, we will all need compassionate, non-judgmental support. We will fill the role of both giver and receiver multiple times as we travel through life's losses, as well as the losses of those we love.

## Why I Wrote This Book

I recently attended a neighborhood social function and was impressed and touched by a couple of retired gentlemen who noticed that their newly widowed neighbor was not in attendance. With compassion, they noted that being a widower "is a new way of life," one that takes time to adapt to all the changes that accompany the loss of a spouse.

They walked to his home to try and coax him to the gathering but returned shortly without him. Within a half-hour, however, he came to the party on his own, responding to his neighbors' kindness and caring.

There are individuals like my neighbors who care deeply about others and do what they can to help those grieving in their social circles, churches and communities. However, many grievers do not have people in their lives who understand the nature of grief.

Many community programs help those who grieve, such as those run by hospice programs and grief centers. However, many grievers will not attend such programs, nor will they avail themselves of counseling, or other types of support. Many will grieve alone.

I wrote this book to address some of the common concerns and experiences that keep people captive, lonely, and feeling crazy in their grief. I wanted to offer a broader picture of grief so that grievers could have a better understanding, not just of grief in general, but of the uniqueness of their personal grief.

I wrote to offer compassion and support in the middle of the night when sleep is elusive, and anxiety is high. My hope is that the information and vignettes of others' grief experiences helps to break down some of the isolation, so many grievers feel.

Although a book cannot hold your hand or tell you, "I am here for you," I hope it provides you inspiration for ways to mourn and care for yourself as you experience grief in your own way and on your own timetable.

### If the Death is Recent

Parts of this book may seem too overwhelming to be of much help if you are newly grieving. Jump ahead to the section on the Common Experiences of Grief and the Myths of Grief first. Educating yourself in these areas alone may help normalize your personal experience of grief. These might be the best places to start.

### If the Loss is Other Than a Death

Although this book is written for those grieving the death of a loved one, all of the feelings, struggles, challenges and coping tactics apply to any of life's losses. You may have experienced divorce, unemployment, or foreclosure, for example. These and other less recognized losses, such as a good friend moving across the country or your child's school closing, can have a tremendous impact on your life. I encourage you to spend some time identifying and mourning these and other losses significant to you.

**My Hope for You**

I hope this book provides you comfort as you persevere with your grief and move through it to a place of renewal, a new landscape, where there is hope and light again. Grieving the way that is natural for you, with few exceptions, is healthy and normal. Time-frames and experiences may vary widely but if you:

- allow grief to be present in your life, in whatever form it takes, without resistance,

- allow yourself to be with your grief, sometimes alone and sometimes with others acting as loving witnesses,

- and care for yourself as you would a dear friend as you learn to take on new roles, you will do more than endure your grief as you move into a new life with your loved one tucked firmly into your heart.

I hope that some of the suggestions in this book will allow you to be with your grief without judgment instead of trying to avoid, change, or outsmart it. Remember that this book's suggestions are possibilities only; anything that does not ring true or make sense to you, please ignore and move on to those that do.

The information offered about how you may experience grief and tactics for coping will hopefully provide you with meaningful ways to care for yourself, honor your loved one, and grow personally. Of course, no one asks for a tragedy to learn and grow! But if you have loved someone, you will grieve their death, and if you are open to it, it is possible to gain wisdom, strength, and peace from even the most devastating of life's losses.  Above all, I wish you courage, strength, healing, and peace as you travel your inner landscape of grief.

Marsha

# CONTENTS

# Chapter One

# THE LAY of the LAND

*Solo Climb*

## THE LONELY LANDSCAPE OF GRIEF

The death of someone we love is one of the most painful events experienced in a lifetime. Intellectually we may know that death happens to all, and yet, the idea is so unthinkable that we often live as if it will not touch ourselves or our loved ones.

The unthinkable has likely happened to you. It doesn't matter whether you got a call at 3:00 am or were present for the death after a long illness: your heart breaks as you face life without someone you love. You have my profound condolences for your loss! You may be looking for answers, relief, and some way to cope with what seems like an insurmountable mountain of grief.

We ignore grief in our death-denying, fast-paced culture. You see, grief takes *attention* and *time*. Life is streamlined and made efficient in so many ways that grieving seems like a burden, an interruption, an inconvenience. In fact, it is all of these things. It is also necessary.

Although you may feel lonely, you are not alone in your grief. With almost 2.9 million deaths annually in the United States alone, each death leaves an average of 4-5 people grieving in its wake.[1] Still, many of us find our time of grief to be a very lonely one. For many people grieving is a solitary activity, but not necessarily by choice. Many people simply do not have a support system. This isolation can lead you to feel as if you are "going crazy."

You are not losing your mind, although grieving can indeed feel crazy-making at times, leaving you heartsick and emotionally and physically depleted. People often report feeling "crazy" when they have little or no control over an experience, but are expected to endure it anyway. Grieving a death is one such experience.

It's no one's fault, really; there are no structures, traditions, or institutions in our culture that recognize, acknowledge, or support those who grieve, much past the visitation, funeral, or memorial service. And many people, for a variety of reasons, are choosing to forgo even these long-held traditions, some for financial reasons and others so they can "remember them the way they were," hoping that they will somehow lessen grief's pain.

A funeral or memorial service are some of the few public rituals available that help us accept the reality of death (an essential task of grieving) and receive the support of others, which is crucial to healing. They serve a critical purpose in times of loss.

In grief, our familiar inner landscape changes. We may feel pain, despair, fear, aimlessness, and loneliness. We may wonder how we will survive, knowing nothing of the customs or currency in this lonely landscape.

Right now, you may even wonder if there is a future for you. You may not even care as you move through the obligations of the day, caring for children, working, going to school, etc. The weight of each day's responsibilities alone may be exhausting for you.

No guide can predict with certainty how you will grieve or how long it will take. What we do know is when we reach that point it will not be like life before the death. A life touched by grief is a changed life. Despite this uncertainty, there are still things you can do for yourself to tend to, nurture, and heal your broken heart.

Over time, with dedicated self-care and the support of caring others, you may begin to experience longer and more frequent moments of contentment and openness to new experiences. As you continue to grieve, you may find yourself spending more time thinking of loving, touching, even funny memories of your loved one and less of the death itself.

Giving attention to your needs, spending regular time with your grief, and seeking support as needed, are indispensable elements to healing your broken heart.

**DEFINITIONS: GRIEF and MOURNING**

Grief is the normal and universal reaction to loss, the very personal array of thoughts, feelings and physical, behavioral and spiritual responses we have after a loved one dies. It is the inward lived experience of loss and as unique as your DNA. Our language is woefully inadequate when it comes to conveying the depth and breadth of personal grief. You may use the same words to describe your grief as someone else enduring a similar loss, and yet, words fail to convey the nuances that distinguish one's grief from another's.

We begin negotiating grief at a very early age. As infants, the moment our parents move out of our sight, we grieve what we cannot have. Going to kindergarten is a significant loss for some children and their parents. Even highly anticipated events, like high school graduation, for example, contain an edge of sadness: for the child who is leaving family, friends, and home for the unknown, as well as for the parents who know that although their child will always need them, things will never be quite the same. It's necessary to identify and mourn these losses as well.

If grief is the inner experience of loss, mourning is the decision to express your grief outwardly, usually influenced by culture, religion, and the history of grieving within our extended families. For some, mourning is limited to the visitation, funeral, wake, or memorial service.

Although all people grieve, not everyone mourns. Mourning is more than expressing one's feelings. In order to integrate this loss into your life you must choose those activities that allow you to express and process your grief.

Mourning may include such things as visiting the grave, scattering the ashes, journaling, art, photography, reminiscing with others about your loved one, or attending a grief support group, for example. Mourning allows us to receive support from others who care. It is this interaction that allows us to transform our grief and move forward with hope. Mourning involves actions that help you make sense of your loss over time, integrate it into your life, and ultimately, find a way to live with it. Grievers working excessive hours to stay busy, or indulging in too much alcohol, drugs, or food, for example, are hoping to circumvent the pain of grief.

There are legitimate reasons why some grievers will avoid mourning. They may be overwhelmed by the enormity of their loss. They may have never seen someone mourn in healthy ways. Or perhaps they have been taught to "just push through". If you are overwhelmed and feel paralyzed or numb, seeing a mental health professional who can support you in this process may be beneficial.

## VISITING the GRAND CANYON: A METAPHOR for the UNIQUENESS of PERSONAL GRIEF

One way to describe personal grief is to compare it with the experience of exploring the Grand Canyon. While visiting there, I noticed that some canyon visitors take an airplane or helicopter ride, viewing the expanse of this incredible wonder, but do not spend much time on the ground at all. Others may travel to the Canyon base by mules trained to walk on the outside of the trail near the edge, definitely not for those afraid of heights! Still, others may take a trip down the river's length at the Canyon's deepest point or forge a rugged path down into the valley, across the river below and make an arduous trip up the other side. Some may take their time and spend many days learning all that the Canyon has to offer, while others may spend an afternoon sitting at the edge in awe before they go on their way. What they saw, felt, heard, and encountered in the landscape will differ for each, but all will have experienced the Grand Canyon.

And so it is with personal grief. Those who avoid going beyond the rim of loss to experience the depths of grief may perceive it as overwhelming and impossible. Others may take side trips into grief, approaching it in time-limited forays only to retreat to higher ground if they become overwhelmed. Some may experience grief in all its forms, allowing it to sweep over them as it comes, without resistance.

Some grievers are patient with themselves, realizing that one cannot rush grief, while others may criticize theselves and ask, "Why am I still feeling this way?" when grief is still raw. What they saw, felt, heard, and encountered in their inner landscape will differ for each, but all will have experienced grief.

## THE PURPOSE of GRIEF

Grieving allows us to expend all that we have invested in our loved one: our love, dreams, future plans, promises, dependencies and life as it was, so we might channel all our inner resources to move into the future with peace. Taking time to mourn allows us time to remember, honor, and, ultimately, say goodbye to what was so that we can accept and make room for what is to be.

In a scene from the movie Shadowlands, C. S. Lewis and his wife Joy (who was diagnosed with terminal cancer) are enjoying a trip while her cancer is in remission. One moment he is full of the joy of their togetherness, and in the next, he realizes the imminence of her death and his grief. Joy tells him, that "What I'm trying to say is the pain, then, is part of this happiness, now. That's the deal." [2]

While we may know intellectually that "that's the deal", that all life ends, that we will all face the grief of physical separation, in the crush of everyday life, we may live as if we have forever. With every death, with every loss, we realize how limited forever is.

Grief is the normal and necessary reaction to loss, and yet we do not expect it despite knowing that we will all face the death of loved ones—as well as our own. Failing to grieve makes future losses complicated. Each loss is layered over those preceding it. Each loss must be mourned, or grieving successive losses becomes more challenging. John W. James and Russell Friedman, from the Grief Recovery Institute, put it best when they wrote: "Unresolved loss is cumulative and cumulatively negative." [3]

Another reason to grieve is that there are often younger, vulnerable ones watching us grieve—and they are learning from our example. What example are we setting?

Grieving in healthy ways is a gift, a legacy, that can impact our families for generations. Our example may be the permission our children and grandchildren need to grieve their losses so they can live well again after loss. Whether we choose to meet grief head-on or attempt to circumvent it, we need to remember that younger eyes are watching.

## THE UNIQUENESS of PERSONAL GRIEF

There is no way to predict with absolute certainty how you will grieve. However, some circumstances will likely influence your personal grief experience. First, look to your previous losses for clues: how have you handled the most significant loss in your life up to this point? How you coped with that loss is often the best predictor of how you will grieve the death of your loved one, although not the only one. Other circumstances that may shape your grief are:

### *Your personal resilience.*

Do you have a history of coping well with life's losses, or have you coped by overindulging in food, alcohol, drugs, gambling, or sex? Have you engaged in overworking or overspending? These unhealthy attempts to side-step grief often create other problems in the long run.

Resilience is the ability to bounce back from life's losses and challenges. It is not necessarily those who have experienced the fewest losses who have the greatest resilience, but those who have weathered many of life's storms and have come back from those losses stronger than before.

Some grievers face life's losses by allowing grief to come and go as it will, seeking support from others as they need it, and taking good care of themselves. Although grieving is never easy, these grievers may find it easier to cope than those who avoid their grief by isolating themselves or using unhealthy means to cope. It takes a lot of energy to grieve, but it takes even more to avoid grief.

### *Your personal loss history.*

Did you experience losses in childhood?

Did you experience or endure several losses in a short period of time?

Have you suffered a sudden or traumatic loss?

Or have you experienced life's expected losses beginning with your elderly grandparents and pets?

In general, those who have experienced losses early in life, multiple losses in a short period of time or a sudden or traumatic loss are at risk for complicated grief. Examples include violent deaths (such as suicide, murder or accidents), the death of a child, or a history of trauma, abuse, or neglect in one's childhood, to name a few.

In complicated grief, there is an extreme focus on the manner of death of the loved one, incapacitating the griever and making it difficult to accept the loss. You may give attention to all that reminds you of your loved one, or you may go to great lengths to avoid any such reminders.

Isolating from others, feeling numb, feeling guilty that you may have contributed to the death (or failed to prevent it) are some of the hallmarks of complicated grief. Such grievers may also become bitter and feel that life no longer has meaning. Many cannot enjoy life or recall enjoyable memories of their loved one, making it difficult to carry out daily responsibilities. Some people are so overwhelmed they become shadows of their former selves.

We learn to grieve in childhood by watching parents or other caregivers grieve, who may or may not have witnessed healthy grieving themselves. Think back to the examples of mourning you witnessed as a child and consider how these may have influenced you.

### *Your current state of health and well-being.*

Are you in relatively good physical and mental health, or do you have chronic health issues? Even a relatively healthy person may experience physical pain and a depressed mood after a death. If you are already dealing with heart disease, anxiety, or depression, or have a history of trauma, for example, grief may strain your ability to cope. Adding the stress of a significant loss to someone whose health is already compromised may make coping extremely challenging.

### *Your outlook on life.*

Do you have a positive outlook on life in general, or do you tend to focus on its negative aspects? If you are a "glass half full" person, someone who focuses on the good that life holds, it may be easier for you to grieve and find meaning in your loss than for someone who sees life as the "glass half empty" focusing on life's deficits.

### The strength of your spirituality.

Do you find meaning and strength in your spiritual beliefs, or are your beliefs unsupportive of your grief? Research has been limited and has not yet definitively proven faith's ability to shore up the griever after a loss. However, most people do turn to their beliefs after a loss to cope. One significant benefit of a connection to a faith community may be ready access to a support system and the growing number of grief ministries becoming available.

### The quality of your support system.

Do you have one or two people with whom you can tell "the good, the bad and the ugly"? Or do you often find yourself alone and isolated? If you have at least one safe person who will listen without judgment and without trying to fix what is unfixable, you are very fortunate. The quality of support received is crucial to healthy coping for grievers.

### The circumstances of the death.

Was the death at the end of an extended illness, or was it sudden and traumatic? An unexpected or traumatic death, one in which there is no time to say goodbye or make amends, is different from one after a long illness. Knowing someone is dying allows us the opportunity to say all the things that need to be said, help prepare oneself for life without them, and tie up loose ends in the relationship as much as possible. When a sudden or traumatic death occurs, the griever is deprived of these opportunities and often left with a multitude of questions and other loose ends.

### The manner of death.

An anticipated death after a long illness or an accident resulting in death is the socially accepted norm of how death occurs in our culture. For deaths due to suicide or overdose (deaths that some may judge as evidence of weak character or moral or spiritual weakness), the griever is often isolated and sometimes ostracized, making it very difficult to ask others for support. It is a sad truth that there is still widespread misunderstanding in our culture regarding mental illness and addiction.

All those grieving a death by any means deserve our compassion and support. In Nickel Mines, Pennsylvania, the Amish community demonstrated this compassion to the world in 2006. A gunman killed five Amish girls and wounded five others in their schoolhouse. The gunman was a local dairy truck driver who then took his own life.

That night representatives of the Amish community walked to the home of the shooter's widow and children as well as to his mother's house. They offered support in their time of grief and said they had forgiven the widow's husband, the mother's son. They wanted the family to stay in the community and not move away in shame. They recognized that they, too, were innocent victims.

### *The history of grief within your extended family and by generation.*

The history of grief within families can have an enormous and often unrecognized impact on losses occurring in the present time. We learn how to mourn at an early age from the examples we witness in our parents and other adults around us. So, whether you have a family history of resilience in the face of loss or one of deep despair and unresolved grief, it will likely influence how you grieve today.

When grief is unacknowledged and unresolved, it may be passed on to our children and grandchildren, affecting their ability to grieve in healthy ways. Demonstrating how to handle difficult emotions, take care of oneself in trying times, and find purpose and hope in life again can contribute to our families' health and resilience for generations to come.

## RITUAL, WRITING, and REMEMBRANCE

Grievers often need more than education and validation to believe that whatever they are feeling is normal. Many feel helpless because they believe there is little they can do about their loss. It is true: we cannot change what has happened.

There are activities, however, that can help grievers experience deeply held feelings, inspire long lost memories, and work through unresolved relationships. These activities can help us acknowledge beginnings, endings, and holidays in ways that heal as well as honor the loved one. These activities involve Ritual, Writing, and Remembrance.

## Ritual and Healing

Grief rituals are activities that symbolically bridge the past and present, and help us remember and honor what was, what is, and sometimes, what is to be. Rituals can be rich in meaning and symbolism, open to our interpretation as ritual-makers, and can be anything we say they are.

When I was growing up, we spent every Memorial Day doing the same thing. My parents would load my sister, brother, and myself in the family station wagon. We'd meet my mother's siblings and their families at the first of many stops to several of the family cemeteries. Clearing the debris around the grave, washing the gravestone, and hand trimming the grass to give it a better frame, were all part of this annual ritual.

My mother would kneel and plant the flowers that would bloom for the summer, standing like sentinels to our loved ones. After the planting, we would sit near the grave and have a picnic lunch.

It was meaningful and respectful, not grim or gruesome. It taught me that death was part of life and that our loved ones live on in our hearts as long as we live. Living far away from the family cemeteries, I still remember with fondness this ritual that gave me a larger sense of family and my place in it.

In our culture, we have special rituals to commemorate a life and acknowledge our ongoing bonds with our deceased loved ones. The most obvious ones are the visitation, funeral, or memorial service; these are likely over for you. Perhaps you or your loved one chose not to have a visitation or service at all.

Research at the Harvard Business School notes the power of personal rituals to increase a sense of control while reducing grief, even if the griever does not necessarily believe in the power of ritual to do so. The rituals noted were personal, and the majority involved no one else.[4]

Some grievers continue to honor the relationship by doing something they always did with their loved one, such as listening to music they had previously enjoyed together or tending the garden, for example.

Some grievers choose to honor a loved one's favorite cause on their behalf such as donating to a favorite charity or participating in a charity fundraiser.

I recently read about a widow who chose to continue her husband's ritual of taking his truck to the car wash weekly as he always did when he was alive.  In doing so, she felt closer to him.

Although these activities are sad, performing them decreased rather than increased their sadness. It seems that rituals also reduce the sense of powerlessness that grievers often feel. If you  wanted  to do  something  but were unable to do so for whatever reason, it is not too late to design your own ritual.

## **<u>Writing and Healing</u>**

I first began to journal when I found myself alone as a single mother. The separation was not something I wanted; I was in shock and terrified, thinking of my future as a stay-at-home mom with two young children. I committed to journaling at least one time daily to monitor what I was feeling and as a way to discharge my stress.

At that time, however, I was not aware of journaling's ability to manifest the magic of insight. I often recommend journaling to clients, having witnessed its impact on clients, and experienced its benefits for myself. Journaling has often helped me discover things that are, at times, a complete revelation when I write them down, revealing things I have not yet told myself.

Journaling is a beautiful trigger for memories. You can note trends in your thoughts and feelings, over time. A review of your journal is the timeline where you share the memoir of your joys, sorrows, challenges, victories, and growth in your life. Going back to read entries after some time has passed is a great way to note personal growth, which is helpful when you feel stuck, and change seems slow at best.

Your grief is worth chronicling. Using journaling as a gauge for your experience with grief may help you stay in touch with thoughts, feelings, wants, needs, and fears that may otherwise remain buried due to the noise and busyness of everyday life. Opening oneself to self-awareness through journaling after a loss can lead to unexpected life lessons that foster wisdom and, ultimately, hope.

You may think, "But I am not a writer." I am here to tell you that you do not have to be. Some may write pages, others may opt for a bullet point format, and still others will do well with a single sentence summarizing their day. Style is not as important as the potential for insight, wisdom, and peace.

Journal prompt suggestions are at the end of the book under Chapter 7, Landscape Tools. If you have decided to write or journal, consider those questions that pertain to your current experience of grief, your interests, and your challenges. If some prompts do not relate to you or your circumstances, skip them. Do not limit yourself to these questions alone; you will likely think of many others. What matters is that you are capturing on paper what is essential for you.

### Remembrance and Healing

How do you wish to remember your loved one? Remembrance serves to celebrate and honor your loved one's memory and is, therefore, both a looking back and a looking forward. Grievers must acknowledge both the good and the not-so-good memories to mourn the whole person. Healing is underway as positive remembrances more frequently occupy your thoughts, with fewer thoughts of the death itself.

One of the biggest fears that grievers have is that others may forget their loved ones. Remembrance is a recalling of cherished memories held deeply in your heart. It can be a tribute to and celebration of all they brought to your life, not only of life's significant events but minor everyday things as well.

I remember "Lynn" a widow who had  spent much of her free time with her husband, enjoying their mutual love of ballroom dancing. I can still picture her smiling as she demonstrated dancing with her invisible partner, clearly recalling the wonderful times she and her husband had spent dancing together.

I have a dear friend "Annie" who lost her mother to Alzheimer's years before she actually died. After her death, she inherited her mothers' pastry cutter which is the old-style metal cutter with a worn handle.  Just as she'd watched her mother do a thousand times, she uses the cutter each time she bakes a pie.  She treasures this pastry cutter not only for the memories it evokes, but because when she holds it, she feels like she's holding her mother's hand.

Bittersweet memories of the common elements of life together are often a part of the  grief  experience. That is where  some of our most  cherished  memories live. Consider ways you can honor your loved one that bring them into your life.

# Chapter Two

# SURVEYING the TERRAIN

*Storm's Coming*

## FIFTEEN MYTHS ABOUT GRIEF

More than anything else, the myths we believe about how grieving should be done keep us captive as we hold to some outdated or unhelpful view of our role as griever.

It is vital to educate oneself about the nature of grief to be free to grieve in the way we need to naturally, without apology or self-recrimination. Knowing the myths of grief will also help us respond to the unhelpful comments of well-meaning others who may promote these out of ignorance. There are many misconceptions about grief. The following are some of the most common.

### 1. Grief is an emotional experience only.

Grief is a whole person experience: body, mind, and spirit. Each domain is connected with and influenced by the others.

Grief experiences can include: intrusive thoughts, physical pain, spiritual anguish, and deep sadness, to name a few. All are normal.

Although more research is needed, the emotional pain caused by grief frequently exhibits itself in physical symptoms. Heart pain, aching joints or muscles are commonly experienced by those grieving a death. No wonder our language is so full of physical metaphors for emotional pain: "My heart is breaking," or "I'm all torn up inside." I am sure you can think of many others.

Did you know it is possible to die of a broken heart? "Broken Heart Syndrome," also known as Stress-Cardiomyopathy, or Takotsubo Cardiomyopathy, occurs when a stress-related event, such as the grief associated with the loss of a loved one, causes a temporary enlargement of part of the heart. The heart then fails to pump properly creating symptoms including angina (intense chest pain) and shortness of breath, even in those with no previous cardiac problems. Although the symptoms may mimic a heart attack, unlike a heart attack, a CT scan for someone who has Broken Heart Syndrome will show no blockage of arteries. It is highly treatable and rarely fatal.[5] If your grief's physical symptoms worsen or if a chronic condition worsens, please see your healthcare provider.

## 2.   Grief takes a very long time to get through.

There is no paved highway around grief. There is no set time frame for the end of grief; grief takes as long as it takes for each person. For some, that will be within a year. For others, it will take much longer. With few exceptions, all are normal.

It is human nature to make comparisons. We define smart by what is ignorant, pretty by what is ugly, kind by what is cruel, etc. Sometimes thoughts come like "My grief is worse than anyone else's," or "Why am I not crying like my sister? Something must be wrong with me." We apply comparisons to time frames for grief as well. Not everyone who remarries in the first year of grief is making a big mistake. Not everyone who carries their grief  publicly for years is most loving. Sometimes we seek comparisons to find common ground with other grievers or to feel normal. Comparisons only hurt grievers. We can seek connection in grief by being respectful of others who grieve differently than we do. We can forge our footpath through grief each day and sometimes learn from those who grieve differently than we do.

## 3.   Grief is done in stages.

Dr. Elizabeth Kubler-Ross's research on the five stages of grief detailed in her book, On Death and Dying, was groundbreaking, yet even she reminded us that it was a theory only and one intended to be applied only to the dying. Somehow it has been applied to every loss, from job loss to hair loss! Sometimes people wonder what stage of grief they are in to determine how close they are to finishing with grief.

Unlike a staging theory, personal grief is not linear; it is up and down, cyclical, and back and forth. In other words, grief is often anything but a steady forward movement. It is no surprise that grievers and grief specialists alike often reference the image of a roller coaster. You may think you have finished a piece of grief only to revisit it months or even years later.

It's okay! You have done nothing wrong. You may be revisiting it because something new has come into your awareness, and there is more to learn, maybe something you were not ready for earlier.

I have met grievers who were angry because others expected specific grief reactions and emotions based on a staging theory that they did not experience. Not only are they grieving, now they feel like they cannot even do that right. Avoid putting yourself into a staging theory; grieve in your unique way and let others do the same.

## 4. It's important to stay busy to get through grief.

Well-meaning family and friends may insist that you get busy, start dating again, take a cruise, or something else they believe will help you get over grief. The problem is that people who stay busy all the time, without taking some time to face their grief often leave it unresolved, only to be overwhelmed by the next significant loss.

Much of the pain of grief is in our resistance to its presence in our lives. If your actions usually take you away from grief, it may be a distraction, a way to divert yourself from the hard feelings of grief. Distractions can help you over a hard day, but it is impossible to side-step grief indefinitely. Having a reason to leave the house, be involved with others, and invest in life again is good, provided there is still room for grieving.

**5.   You must get rid of all reminders of your loved one as soon as possible.**

Being surrounded by things that remind you of your loved one, such as photos, voice recordings, hand-made objects, souvenirs from travels, and other such mementos, may give a sense of closeness and consolation at a time it is most needed.

For example, wearing or sleeping with an article of clothing because it retains the scent of your loved one is very common. Our sense of smell evokes the quickest and most potent memories. Processed within the part of the brain that stores emotional memories, forever links the scent with the memory. I still associate the scent of gardenias with my grandmother's visitation, which occurred almost 60 years ago.

These precious memories may help us transition our connection to our loved one based on physical presence to one based on our continued love in memory and spirit.

Of course, you will want to keep some special items close to you simply because they comfort you and make you smile. Unless you have a mansion or a storage unit, however, keeping everything may not be practical. Decide what you want to keep and what you want to give to other family members, special friends, a charity or possibly sell, in your own time.

Unless you are under a deadline, you can tackle cleaning the home, room, or closet when you are ready; there is no set timetable. If you need or want to do it yet feel overwhelmed, solicit the help of an organized friend who will likely be grateful to know there is a concrete way they can help and support you.

### 6. It is best not to make any significant decisions in the next year.

It is okay to make decisions in the first year after a loss, provided you are clear about your motives. While it is true that some people may have a knee-jerk reaction to unloading their home quickly because it holds too many memories, many other people are logical and practical about their needs. They may even benefit from a change of environment. Ask yourself, "what do I hope to accomplish by selling my home right now?" If you have legitimate financial or necessary relocation reasons, then, by all means, sell. If you want to move to escape memories, however, you may find that they follow you wherever you go.

A more serious concern is choosing to move prematurely into a new relationship. It is essential to know that the feelings associated with romantic love may convince some grievers that their grief is indeed gone. If you are thinking of remarrying, consider, "why do I want to marry this person now?" If your honest answer is: "Because I cannot stand being alone" or "I am afraid I will be alone for the rest of my life," you may be wise to sit with and consider things further before making a final decision. Seek the counsel of trusted family and friends, leaders in your faith community, or a counselor who can help you sort out your feelings.

No one likes to be lonely, and it is okay to enjoy someone's company. If you feel a sudden diminishing of your grief when you engage in a new relationship, however, the relief you feel may only be temporary. Approach new relationships with caution and wisdom.

### 7. If I am grieving, something must be wrong.

Sometimes people think a resurfacing of earlier emotions signifies a problem. I remember "Madelyn," a widow I worked with who criticized herself for not moving ahead as she thought she should. When she was reminded that it had only been a few months since her husband's death, she was relieved. She needed to remind herself of this when she pressured herself to be done prematurely with her grief.

The nature of grief may include times when we revisit emotions experienced previously. Revisiting is very common and does not mean we have moved back to the first day of grief. Revisiting is okay—and normal.

## 8.   Those who grieve harder and longer, or more openly, must love more  deeply than others.

Sometimes grief seems to be a competition between people, each trying to prove how close they were and how much they loved. You cannot compare grief; the relationship you had with your loved one was unique and different from any other relationship, even if the relationship appears similar.

For example, if a mother of five dies, she leaves behind five unique relationships and five grievers with their unique grief responses. They may have similar grieving styles, but the intensity, the nature of the grief experience itself, and who the mother was to them personally will be different for each one.

When we grieve, it is because we have loved. Keep the focus on what you each share in grief and otherwise allow the other to grieve in their own way without judgment.

## 9.  Self-pity is to be avoided at all costs.

Why does our culture allow us to feel sympathy for others and not for ourselves? I have met people at workplace debriefings following a death who are isolated (mainly due to caregiving responsibilities) and have no confidant. Some have been shamed into believing that self-pity is the ultimate sin.

Healthy self-pity is feeling sorry for yourself when there is no one else to do so, or do so in a way that acknowledges the depth of your loss. Feeling compassion for yourself, feeling self-pity in moderation, is more than okay; it is healing. Healthy self-pity says, "Of course, I'm sad, I've lost the love of my life! " or "My heart is broken! I cannot believe my child has died !" Who else understands the magnitude of your loss better than you do? Having a good cry for yourself can release pent-up emotion, produce relaxation, and increase your compassion for others.

Like anything else that is good when done in moderation, self-pity can cross over into unhealthy territory if it becomes obsessive and is used as an excuse not to do what you can for yourself or to manipulate others. It may become an issue if you become stuck in the stories in your head that tell you, "You will always be alone," or "Why do things like this always happen to me? " or "God is punishing me" or other destructive messages. Second, only to the cruel things well-meaning others say to us are the cruel and untrue things we tell ourselves. Compassion is okay; self-punishment is not.

### 10.  Expressing anger about your loved one is speaking ill of the dead.

Your relationship with your loved one does not end with death. Many grieving people have unresolved relationship issues at death, just as they did when their loved one was alive. You may feel angry that your loved one has abandoned you through death, even though your logical mind tells you they did not choose to do so.

Grief is not logical; it just is. It is okay to be angry and talk about your anger with safe people, such as compassionate family, friends, or a spiritual adviser. It is also okay to tell your loved one of your thoughts and feelings. You cannot hurt them; they cannot hurt you. It is okay to speak the truth in love.

Suppressing feelings can cause them to re-emerge through physical symptoms and disease. I remember "Jake," a client whose spouse had died after a long battle with an illness she contracted in young adulthood. Jake had developed chronic digestive issues after "Mary" died. I could feel the anger Jake was suppressing in our first visit; it was palpable. He needed to keep up a façade of "I'm fine" and did not want to discuss his grief experience in any detail. If you feel anger, it is essential to acknowledge it and find safe ways to channel it.

## 11. Feeling angry with God over your loss is sacrilegious.

After a significant loss, the foremost question in the griever's mind is, "Why"? Although some questions may be answered factually, "Why did this happen?" cannot be answered satisfactorily.

"Why" is a profoundly spiritual question that presupposes that Someone or something had the power to prevent or change the course of events. Even those who do not consider themselves very spiritual ask, "Why?" It is a universal question. "Why did my loved one die?" "Why did my loved one have to suffer?" "Why did the doctor miss the diagnosis?"

A genuine and trusting relationship requires honesty and being oneself. A relationship with God is no different. Talking to God (God as you experience God) in anger, peace, sadness, happiness, despair, or hope, telling God your experience in your own way, is the hallmark of an authentic relationship. Go ahead and tell God exactly how you feel.

## 12. You must say goodbye to your loved one to let go.

I have met very few people who do not have an ongoing relationship of some type with their deceased loved one. Telling your loved one about problems in your day-to-day life, about the joys in life that you wished they could be there for, or thinking, "what would Ray do?" are very common experiences for grievers. The connection—the love you feel for your beloved— will never die.

When my father died, my then nine-year-old son told me, "Now Grandpa is always with me." He intuitively understood the continuing connection, as children often do.

Research has demonstrated that a continued connection not only provides consolation but allows the griever to create a new relationship with the loved one, based on love and memory, allowing them to move into a new life.

Believing that your connection and love are still there is normal; however, limiting your relationships with the living because of your relationship with your deceased loved one is problematic. Saying goodbye to life as you knew it with your loved one is a critical part of healing. Fortunately, saying goodbye to the love and the continued connection is not.

### 13.  If I let go of my grief, I will let go of the love and my loved one.

This is a myth that we may not voice to anyone —maybe not even to ourselves.

You may fear that in moving past your grief, there will be nothing to replace it. At least your sadness, tears, and anger tell you that you are still connected to your loved one, if only through your pain. Some may also fear that moving past grief is to forget their loved one.

It is a powerful experience to feel connected to someone you cannot see with your eyes, but know is still with you. Helen Keller, born blind and deaf, certainly knew grief and isolation. She said this about loss: "What we once enjoyed and deeply loved, we can never lose, for all that we love deeply becomes a part of us." [6]    The nature of your relationship may change, but the love you shared will remain.

## 14.    Getting thorough the first year is the hardest.

There is nothing magical about getting through the first year of grief. Grief is not only confined to the first year after death. Frequently the second-year dawns, and with it, the realization that this loss is forever.

We need ongoing caring support in our grief, the knowledge that others understand that there is no need to push or rush us, that it is indeed normal to grieve for as long as we need to without apology.

## 15.    Grief is forever.

There is no "getting over" the death of someone we love. If "getting over" grief means forgetting and not caring anymore, why would anyone want that? The truth is that we will never stop missing and loving our loved ones. They are irreplaceable, one of a kind.

Loving someone (whether alive or dead) lasts a lifetime. We will continue to have moments of sadness and yearning for our loved ones the rest of our lives. In time, and with attention given to mourning, the hard grief will give way to more extended periods of peace, feeling lighter and not so heavy-hearted, as we learn to live with our loss. Most of us don't "get over" our grief, but learn to live with it over time. At some point we will likely open to new life experiences and relationships while never forgetting the bond that is still there.

Grieving is not the end of love, but rather a transition as we learn to reconnect to that love in new ways. Grief is renegotiating life and learning who you are now without that person's physical presence. Grievers may experience occasional acute episodes of grief, especially around anniversaries of the final illness or death or milestones such as births, graduations and weddings. You may also revisit grief as you age and go through life's developmental phases, thinking about the loss from an older, wiser perspective. If you allow grief to enter your life, its intensity will likely wane over time as you learn to live with your loss.

## WALKING THROUGH GRIEF

To walk through grief means to mourn in such a way that you not only experience feelings of grief, but that you use healthy coping skills to help you transition and adjust to your new life without that person's presence. It means recognizing and experiencing the pain of your loved one's absence and the many ways you will need to change to adapt to this new life. And since it is a walk and not a race, we have to be patient with ourselves. Acceptance plays a role in walking through grief. As we mourn our loved one's death over time, acceptance often increases as grief subsides. It is a byproduct of mourning. Here are some examples of what acceptance is not:

- Acceptance does not mean that the you are "ok" with the death.

- Acceptance does not mean that you no longer care about your loved one.

Accepting "what is" over time, and not what we wish it would be, is a crucial element of walking through grief. The following are some of the realities that must be acknowledged and accepted.

## Acceptance of the Death

Part of healthy grieving is accepting the loss as permanent. Acceptance means we understand that death has occurred and that we realize our loved one is not returning.

For some, inner wrestling occurs as they revisit the illness or accident with hope for a different outcome.

Grief is not logical, and while we may know that it is not possible to change the outcome, it may not keep our minds from trying. We may know intellectually that our loved one is gone, but there is often a time when we continue some daily habits instinctively as if they are still here. This automatic response usually occurs around those activities that are a habit or daily ritual, which we do without even thinking about it.

An example would be reaching for the phone to make a daily check-in call with your loved one as you acclimate to their physical absence. It is not the same thing as denial, which is a protective mechanism that shields us from the terrible reality of grief until we can accept it. Forgetting that you only need to set three table settings is normal. Deciding to set the table for four anyway may be a way of avoiding the reality of grief.

Acceptance of the death can be difficult when your relationship has been everything you had hoped it would be. You may notice people around you who are in contentious relationships or have lost touch over some long-forgotten issue. Yet death has ended your special relationship. As one young husband whose wife died of brain cancer put it, "I don't understand; we got along so well and did so much together. "Why her? Why us? "

Likewise, death can be difficult to accept if your relationship has been less than what you hoped it would be. When all the efforts to come closer have failed or hope that the future will be different ends in death, it can be tough to accept.

I remember a teenager named "Lily" whose mother was dying. She never knew her father and had quite a chaotic and lonely childhood, her mother frequently absent due to drug addiction.

Our work together focused on helping her cope with her sadness and her awareness that her hope for authentic mothering would end with her mother's impending death. When Lily's mother died, her spontaneous response to the news was, "She was the best mother in the world!" This temporary denial allowed her time to accept the reality of her loss and that the special mother-daughter relationship she longed for would never happen.

Accepting your dashed hopes, the death of your dream, takes time. It may take much reflection to reach acceptance and integrate this new reality into your life. Lily was able to do this in time with the support of caring adults that stepped forward to care for her.

Here are some activities that many grievers have found helpful as they adjust to their new reality.

### Participating in funeral or memorial rituals.

A funeral or memorial underscores the reality of death and its permanence and is the beginning of acceptance. This includes viewing the body, if at all possible. Sometimes when grievers choose to have no service or do not view the body, often citing their desire to remember them "as they were", it may foster fantasies that the loved one is still out there somewhere.

In general, viewing the body helps to accept the death; however, this is not true in all cases. In certain deaths where there may have been trauma to the body, for example, it is best to ask the funeral staff to describe what you may see to help you decide if you want to view your loved one.

### Accepting condolences and support from others.

Having a funeral or memorial service is a formal opportunity to receive support from others. Support can extend beyond the funeral or memorial service through social gatherings, cards, and phone calls.

### Visiting and tending to the grave or scattering ashes.

Even those who choose not to have a funeral or memorial service or to view their loved one's body can help themselves heal by visiting the burial site. Some people enjoy the special connection they feel at the grave and the solitude of the cemetery itself. Many choose to bring flowers, notes, or small personal objects, for example. Other grievers, however, may find no special connection with their loved one at the gravesite. There are other ways to honor their loved one at home, enhancing their connection by planting a tree or installing a garden stone, for example. It does not matter what it is as long as it gives meaning and comfort.

## Acceptance of Your Personal Encounter with Grief.

Coping well with grief is not the absence of sadness, anger, tears, wandering thoughts, or spiritual pain. Instead, coping with grief is the absence of resistance to these and other ways grief is experienced. Accepting the terrible reality of loss is counterintuitive in our Western culture, which teaches that one can avoid most pain.

I remember "Curtis," whose sister died at a relatively young age. Curtis had many responsibilities at home and work. He pushed his grief down and worked hard, and raised his family, not realizing that his grief over his sister's death was not gone, but dormant. When his cat died six years later, the intensity of his grief helped him realize he was not only grieving his pet's death but the loss of his sister for the first time.

Sometimes grievers struggle, thinking that something must be wrong if they are feeling bad. To encounter your personal grief, you must have a willingness to explore intense emotions, thoughts, and sensations without judgment and make time to do so. Giving grief its due allows the pain to move through you.

Grief cannot be rushed, avoided, or eliminated, so resistance only delays the inevitable. If you allow yourself to experience your grief, however your grief shows up for you, it will make it easier to grieve subsequent losses without complications. If experiencing these emotions seems like doing surgery on yourself without the benefit of anesthesia, seek out a counselor to help you in this process

## Acceptance of Your Changed Personal life.

It is not only the physical absence of our loved ones that changes our life; that is hard enough. It is the corresponding ways that we must change and adapt in their absence. Our schedule, behavior, activities, responsibilities, social and family roles, etc., are all impacted. Some needed changes will be readily apparent, and some will dawn on us over time as we become more aware of the various roles our loved one played in our life.

Each role must be identified and mourned—roles such as Breadwinner, Ms./Mr. Fix-It, Social Secretary, Financial Planner, Cook, Child Care Provider, or Best Friend, for example, are just a few of many roles your loved one may have played in your life. There are also more subtle roles such as Advocate, Mentor, Protector, or Truth-Sayer, which may be lost with the death.

I remember a friend, "Emma", who acknowledged that acceptance in her family changed with her brother's death. For as long as she could remember she was treated as an outcast for reasons unknown to her. Her brother insisted on her inclusion in all family activities, which had not always happened without his support. With his death, she was left without her advocate and grieved his death deeply.

"Sophia," a young widow, considered her husband, her "Shell Answer Man". She depended on him to know a little something about everything and his ability to fix anything. His sudden death required that she step up and hire someone to care for all the things she could not do herself. However, she could not replace her in-house Shell Answer Man and grieved this intensely.

## CONTINUING YOUR CONNECTION

The heart searches and yearns for our loved ones to make real again what is still so very real in our hearts. Part of the work of grief is to continue the relationship but in a new way. As we start each day, we say goodbye to those we live with and take a representation (such as an image or memory) of them with us for the day. Many of our living relationships are carried out in our hearts and memory already due to distance and circumstance.

Our oldest daughter has called her father numerous times to say, "I can't believe your words came out of my mouth today; you're in my head! " We are in each other's heads and hearts and memory already. Deceased loved ones remain a part of us as long as we live.

A widower named "Calvin" deeply grieved the loss of his beloved wife of 37 years. He remembered her in his garden, setting a bench engraved with her name and surrounded by her favorite flowers. Sitting on the bench in the garden, taking in the blossoms' aroma helped Calvin feel closer to her. He spoke with her there, telling her about his day, the grandkids' activities, and asking for her continued guidance.

Death may have separated you physically, but it does not end your relationship. When a loved one dies, it is natural to seek ways to keep your connection alive and hold close to the love that continues to be so dear. Letting go of the in-person relationship, but not the love, is an essential aspect of healing. Letting go is done in one's own time at one's own pace.

Botanists have found a winter rye plant with the world's longest root system measuring up to 387 miles long! Like that winter rye plant, enduring love runs deep and long. Despite their physical absence, our loved ones continue in our hearts in a profound and lasting way.

### FINDING MEANING IN YOUR LOSS

Most of us grapple with the question, "Why did this happen?" Whether you believe in a divine plan for life, a philosophy of life ("all things happen for a reason"), or a belief in nothing beyond the physical world, we look for some meaning in what seems so very meaningless. Finding meaning does not mean we are looking for justification for our loved one's death; there isn't any. It also does not mean that the death was worth any side benefits we may find; it isn't. It does mean that we have found a way to think about our lives in light of our loss and make something positive from it, for ourselves, and sometimes for others.

At some point, most grievers will assign meaning to the death. Some people, however, assign meaning *for* the death such as, "God is punishing me for (fill in the blank)." This type of meaning-making is both unhealthy and unhelpful. Exploring these beliefs with someone you trust from your faith community or with a counselor or therapist may help.

Meaning-making is all about love, honor, and the enduring bond we share with our loved ones. People do this in various ways, and it is as unique to your loved one as it is to you, the meaning-maker.

"Lily," the bright young woman whose mother had died, found that she could find meaning in her loss by participating in cancer fundraisers and awareness campaigns. In doing so, she was able to honor her mother as the one who gave her life and channel her grief into meaningful activities that helped others.

"Samuel," a widower, reported that part of his healing came in finding meaning in the loss of his wife "Grace" by transcribing her life story from conversations they had over time. In doing so, he continued to hear her voice through her own words.

I watched a TV show focusing on the theme of forgiveness, demonstrating a powerful example of meaning-making after a loss. A mother whose son was killed found her meaning travelling the country doing speaking engagements to promote the power of forgiveness—with her son's murderer. This forgiveness did not happen overnight and was not arrived at easily, but it did happen.

You may remember Candy Lightner, the founder of MADD (Mothers Against Drunk Driving), a highly publicized example of meaning-making. Candy found the meaning in her daughter's death by ensuring that other families would not have to go through the trauma and heartache that she did.

Less publicized but no less meaningful are the Annual Golf Fundraisers to conquer cancer, SIDS, or ALS, for example, in a loved one's name.

Although we may not be able to impact our loved one's life anymore, we may be able to impact and help someone else that we have not even met yet, perhaps in a new friendship or volunteer capacity, for example. What matters is finding some way to make meaning in life again for oneself despite the seeming meaninglessness of the loss.

Sometimes when the death seems particularly meaningless (as in a sudden traumatic death or the death of a young person, for example), grievers may be able to find meaning in the life their loved one lived. Was there a particular passion or cause your loved one embraced?

Perhaps you can be involved with that passion or cause in their honor by using your time, talent, or treasure. People do it all the time, even those who didn't think they would ever survive their grief.

The following quote is from Viktor Frankl, a psychiatrist, and author who survived the Nazi death camps then learned that his entire family perished, except for his sister. His yet-to-be-published manuscript representing his entire life's work was taken from him. Despite living in such extreme conditions, Dr. Frankl found that it is still possible to find meaning in the most miserable and dehumanizing experiences. He realized that "In some way, suffering ceases to be suffering at the moment it finds a meaning."[8] Be open to the meaning in your loss and to opportunities to honor your loved one.

## CONCRETE WAYS TO GRIEVE

The idea that there are healthy ways to help grievers mourn seems to baffle many people. Some have been raised with the concept of "keeping a stiff upper lip" after a death of a loved one, or the "you must keep busy" mantra grievers so often hear. "Keeping a stiff upper lip", or holding your grief inside can result in illness and "keeping busy" is only a temporary way to avoid the pain of grief. Neither are healthy approaches to grief and can cause serious problems in the long run. Fortunately, there are some activities that lend themselves to helping us move through and integrate our loss into our lives.

## Mindfulness Meditation

Many people live their entire lives focused on the future or the past. Anxiety takes one into a future that may never happen, and depression takes one into a past that cannot be changed. Focusing on the future or the past means we cannot be fully in the present moment. If done to an extreme, people facing death often feel they've missed out on life.

Mindfulness meditation is paying attention to what is occurring in the present moment. You will observe whatever thoughts, feelings, and sensations that arise without judgment. Mindfulness Meditation is one way to be present with grief.

To begin mindfulness meditation, choose a place in your home where you can be alone in quiet, preferably at the same time each day. Make sure this spot is free from distractions. First, sit comfortably in your chair and close your eyes, allowing your focus to be on your breath. Focus on the sensations as air comes into the nose or as it exits the lips. Breathe as you normally do; you do not have to breathe in any particular way.

Your mind will begin to wander, and thoughts will come and go naturally. Thoughts in this context are words, sentences, impressions, images, feelings, memories, or sensations. Allow your thoughts to come and go; there is no need to push them away or hold onto them. The goal is not to understand or eliminate your thoughts, (which isn't possible) or to troubleshoot a problem. Instead, note these thoughts but do not censor or judge them. As the thought dissipates, bring your focus back to your breathing until the next thought comes.

In the beginning, your thoughts may come rapidly, one on top of another. Some will be about grief, while others may be about mundane things like grocery shopping, for example. All you are trying to do is be present to your thoughts as you experience them in real-time. Accept your thoughts without judgment, including those that may frighten you, such as "I'll always feel this way," or "No one will ever love me again," for example. You will begin to notice a reduction in anxiety or fear over time as you realize that thoughts are not facts.

Spend 5 minutes daily for the first week in mindfulness meditation. Increase your time by an additional 5 minutes each week until you spend 20-30 minutes daily, or at a minimum, several times weekly. Be sure to set a timer so you do not have to look at a clock. Such a practice will reap many positive benefits for your health.

## Creating a Sacred Space

Another way to spend time with your grief is by creating a sacred space. Have a table, shelf, or box to gather pictures, letters, and other special memorabilia next to your chair to inspire you during this time. Accept any memories that come to you as well as the accompanying thoughts or feelings. If nothing comes to you, perhaps one of the following suggestions will spark some:

- Looking at photo albums or videos of your life together.

- Reading old letters or emails from your loved one.

- Playing music that reminds you of your loved one.

- Looking at memorabilia from travel, graduations, baptisms, and other special events.

- For some, journaling or poetry may help express what seems inexpressible.

People are sometimes afraid of their feelings and look to avoid any associated pain. It may be counterintuitive, but it takes more energy to resist pain than to focus on it. Instead of resisting the pain of grief, focus on it directly, and lean into your pain. Leaning into and allowing yourself to experience the pain leads to a release and, ultimately, freedom when done over time.

This works because you are giving your full attention to thoughts, emotions and physical sensations in real time. Being present with "what is" without censorship or judgement allows us to become self-aware, learn life lessons and face future life challenges with wisdom. It's okay to be afraid if you are doing this for the first time. It gets easier with practice.

There is nothing else to do except to allow whatever thoughts and feelings come and wash over you without holding onto them, pushing them away, or minimizing them. The only way to do it wrong is to prevent yourself from feelings and thoughts that occur naturally in your grief. If you feel overwhelmed by grief, try skipping two or three days to give some space in your week for other things between sessions.

For those grieving primarily in a cognitive way, spending time problem-solving ways to manage change and the associated anxiety may be helpful.

I remember a client named "Bob" who became quite anxious when his wife of 55 years died after a long illness. After some thought he decided that perhaps playing the piano (something he had always wanted to try) would be a good distraction from his anxiety. At 70 years old he began teaching himself learning notes and scales on YouTube and practicing daily on the piano his children had played during their childhood lessons. It was the most enjoyable part of his day and a reprieve from all the decisions, paperwork and changes he would need to make.

Some grievers avoid and fear this alone time, afraid of what it might demand from them. It is natural to pull your hand away from the fire, to prevent the pain of grief. Grief may go underground, but will likely reappear, demanding even more attention, after the next loss. Spending time with grief now is critical to healing and the ability to cope with future losses.

If experiencing such feelings alone seems terrifying, seek out the services of a mental health professional who can help you through this process. It may also be a good idea to seek support  through local and online grief support groups to hear how others in similar situations are coping.

# Chapter Three

# COMMON GROUND

*Into the Woods*

## COMMON EXPERIENCES of GRIEF

Although each person's grief is different, some reactions occur often enough to be considered commonplace experiences. Grief impacts your whole person: cognitively, physically, emotionally, behaviorally, and spiritually. The following list notes some of the more common grief reactions.

### Cognitive Changes

- Loss of interest in the world around you
- Intrusive thoughts of the death
- Distraction or the inability to concentrate

- Short-term memory loss
- Sense of unreality
- Difficulty making decisions
- Preoccupation with your loved one

**Physical Changes**
- Extreme fatigue
- Dry mouth
- Muscle weakness
- Changes in eating habits: Over-eating or eating too little
- Changes in sleeping habits: sleeping too much or not being able to fall asleep or stay asleep
- A heightening or deadening of the senses
- Rapid heart rate
- Tightness in the chest or throat
- Aches and pains in the head, neck, or stomach
- Weakened immune system
- Hypersensitivity to noise
- Breathlessness
- Heavy sighs
- "Broken Heart" Syndrome/Stress Cardiomyopathy

**Emotional Changes**
- Deep longing and yearning
- Relief at the end of suffering
- Relief at the end of caregiving

- Anger at the medical profession
- Anger at the insurance company
- Anger at your loved one for abandoning you
- Euphoria at honoring caregiver promises
- Loneliness, a sense of not fitting in
- Fear of the unknown
- Fear of not making it on your own
- Fear of who will die next
- Distrust of others
- Anxiety
- Depressed mood
- Numbness
- Peace at accomplishing what you set out to do
- Regret
- Guilt
- Helplessness
- Unchecked self-pity

## Behavioral Changes

- Isolating from others
- Avoiding places, music, and other reminders of your loved one
- Seeking out places and reminders of your loved one
- Avoidance of or disinterest in sex
- Vivid dreams of your loved one
- Working too much or staying too busy in hopes of avoiding grief

## Spiritual Changes

- Feeling distant from faith
- Increased conviction of faith
- Questioning of beliefs
- Anger at God
- Doubt
- Renewal of faith

## COMMON QUESTIONS ABOUT GRIEF

Below you will find some off the most frequently asked questions about grief.

### 1. How will I grieve?

There are two basic grieving styles: one is primarily through the emotions, such as sadness and tears, and the other is cognitive, with the griever problem-solving and otherwise troubleshooting grief's challenges.

The majority of us grieve in a combination of the two styles, with one being more predominant. To consider what your unique style is, think about the worst experience you have ever had to deal with in your life until now: how did you experience grief? What helped you cope? What did not work? Did you allow time for grief, or did you cope by staying busy as much as possible?

Now think about what helped you cope: was it healthy or harmful? Healthy approaches to grieving do not put your health and well-being or that of others in jeopardy.

Harmful coping methods are bids to do the impossible: circumvent pain and avoid grief.

Two of the most common responses from grievers when asked, "How did you cope with your grief from previous losses?" are "I worked more" or "I drank more." These are honest responses but not practical long-term approaches. These avoidance strategies postpone grief and can create their own set of long-term problems. Take some time to understand your grieving pattern and if necessary, make a choice to grieve in healthy ways. Seek support to do so if needed.

## 2. How long will I grieve?

It is critical to know that time alone does not heal. What you do with that time, however, is essential to healing and renewal.

Coping in healthy ways, accepting your grief's expression and time frames, resisting comparisons with grieving others, and embracing your loss lessons, will allow you to walk through grief and ultimately create a new life. Grieving is a process; the fact that it happens over time is secondary to what we *do* in our time of grief.

The length of time we grieve will depend on many things, varying significantly from person to person. This uncertainty can be unsettling, even frightening, for those who simply want to know when it will be over. Intense grieving may go on for a year or longer and may wax and wane over time.

You will mourn in your own way, meaning that your feelings, thoughts, and time frames will be yours alone. Remember that if the death was sudden or traumatic, this could lengthen grieving significantly. Go ahead and grieve your way—that is what "good grief" is.

### 3. Should I consider professional help? If yes, what should I look for in a counselor?

Most research on grieving suggests that the best support available to you is in your social circles. However, those closest to us may not always be able to help. Consider contacting a therapist, counselor or mental health professional specializing in grief to help you understand and better manage your grief:

- Any time you have thoughts of harming yourself or others.

- Months are passing, and your grief is as intense as it was when the death occurred.

- You experience continued and undiminished fears related to life changes, illness or death.

- You are not functioning in your day-to-day life and neglecting your family, friends, self-care, or other interests that have been meaningful to you.

- Trusted others tell you they see little or no adjustment to your circumstances.

- Anytime you think you should see one.

Remember that those who have suffered a sudden traumatic loss will likely have a longer road through grief, especially if they must deal with the legal system, provide care for family members, have a significant change in income, etc. Getting professional support through that long and sometimes winding road is recommended.

Look for a social worker (MSW), professional counselor, or psychologist licensed in your State. When a professional is "licensed," it means they have met the criteria of their profession (including adhering to a Code of Ethics) as well as criteria the State deems vital to protect the public who may use such services. Each State will have a website where you can check out who is licensed.

In a large metropolitan area, you may be able to find a professional who specializes in grief therapy, but this will likely not be available in smaller areas. However, all professionals listed on the Psychology Today

Find-A-Therapist website, for example, will list issues with which they work. Make sure grief is listed.

To find a therapist with additional training in a specific technique like EMDR (Eye Movement Desensitization and Reprocessing) used for trauma, or Complicated Grief Therapy, look for that information on Psychology Today's Find-a-Therapist website or call your insurance company and ask who they can recommend in your area. Your healthcare professional or a friend may also be an excellent source of referrals. Just remember that a friend may have received therapy for an issue other than grief.

I often talk with prospective clients by phone to answer their questions and give them a sense of who I am and how I work. I encourage you to contact the prospective therapist directly to ask your questions before you go. Finally, be sure to ask if they take your insurance if you plan on using yours.

At your first session, pay attention to the connection you are making with the therapist: do you feel comfortable talking with them? Do you feel they are listening well to your concerns? The best predictor of successful outcomes in therapy is the rapport you have with your therapist. If something seems off, trust your instincts and try another therapist.

Throughout the book I note circumstances that would benefit from working with a mental health professional.

## 4. How will I survive?

Surviving is often the goal of grievers initially, especially when an unknown future looms large, and we feel trapped on grief's rollercoaster.

For some, surviving that first year becomes a goal. "It will be easier if I can get past the holidays" or "I will feel so much better if I can just get past this first year" are common sentiments. Sadly, this goal is achieved without a prize, as the second year unfolds and, along with it, the realization that the loss is permanent.

In and of itself, survival only means that we have outlived a significant loss or tragedy; it says nothing of creating a life of meaning and living well in that new life, something that our loved ones would want for us. Right now, you may not be able to imagine, let alone want, a different life. That is okay; you may not be ready yet to look ahead. Perhaps what is needed is today's small steps. At some point, you will find yourself looking forward more and more.

You have likely experienced many of life's losses and have many coping tools in your toolbox. Think about any change you have had to make previously, such as moving, starting a new job, or attending a new school. At first, everything seems foreign and strange. You may have even considered giving up, fearing you could not manage the unfamiliarity. Grieving a death can be incredibly challenging as your experience of the world, of safety, love, of life itself is shaken hard by death. Use what you have learned from previous experience and consider what may be helpful for you now.

### 5. Will grief take over my life?

After a significant loss, it may be hard to remember that there is still much within your control. Although you could not prevent the death, you can choose to focus on how you spend time with your grief; how you care for yourself and your family; when to humble yourself to let others help; and at some point, how you decide to live the rest of your life. It's important to remember that you are not your grief!

### 6. Who will help me?

Everyone needs someone to talk to at times, and this is especially true when you are grieving. It is vital to make sure that you share with safe people who will listen with compassion and without judgment. You may already know who among your family or friends will fill this role for you. For others, finding someone to listen well may be a challenge.

We need caring witnesses to our grief. Having someone being fully present and actively listening without judgment gives them something to do and removes the pressure to relieve our pain. Ironically, it is in the sharing of suffering that healing begins. So, where do you find a caring witness?

Look around you: who is the best listener that you know?

In whose presence do you find peace? Who will respect your grief without trying to fix it? Who has earned the honor of hearing what your heart has to say?

Look everywhere: they may be at work, in your social circle, at your church, or in your neighborhood. Many grievers have found support through fellow grievers they have met at hospice and community grief support groups. I recall a group of widowers who met in a support group and continued to meet long after the support group ended, having found the unique camaraderie of others who have "been there."

As much as we need help doing things in the wake of a death, simply being there is even more critical. It is ideal to have several people to speak with, but even one person listening well is helpful.

If you want to speak with someone about your loss and do not have a person like this in your life, a mental health professional specializing in grief may be helpful. The most important thing is to use discretion and be selective about whom you talk with as you grieve; what you have to share is precious.

### 7.  How do I respond to well-meaning but hurtful comments?

We do not teach people how to be present with those grieving a loss in our culture. Despite this, many people with good intentions offer suggestions to cope with loss, possibly thinking that you need help if you allow yourself to mourn openly.

The term "grief police" has been coined to name such people. The grief police are everywhere. There are times when I am still shocked by some of the unintentionally cruel remarks people report others have said to them. Mostly, it is well-meaning people who unknowingly hurt grievers with platitudes like, "Now you have an angel in heaven" or "You can always marry again" or "You will have other children." Relationships are unique, one of a kind; they are not interchangeable nor replaceable. These philosophical approaches do not soothe the longing and pain held in the deepest recesses of the heart.

People usually mean well, but many simply do not know what to say, have not yet experienced a devastating loss, or have and did not allow themselves to grieve. If someone makes such a statement to you, it is okay to remain silent without feeling you have to respond. It is also okay to respond honestly with a statement such as, "You may mean well, but that does not help me right now."

### 8. Is my grief normal?

In my professional experience, this question remains mostly unspoken, yet it is a critical question that most grievers want answered. Many suffer in silence. As if dealing with your loss was not hard enough, it can be agonizing to be isolated by these concerns. So, what IS normal?

Think of normal and complicated grief as a continuum that ranges in intensity and persistence of symptoms over time. How you mourn may involve sadness and tears, anger and rage, depression, or apathy. It may also involve euphoria, peace, contentment, and hope, among many other emotions.

Sometimes you may experience some or several of these reactions all in the course of a day. You may also experience periods when you are focused on one emotion only. Some feelings may be with you intensely for a time and then begin to wane. Sometimes such feelings may surprise you by reappearing much later near an anniversary or holiday. These are all a normal part of the grieving process and can vary significantly from griever to griever.

Let me give you one example of the range of grief. Many people have sensory experiences of their loved ones after the death: they see, feel, hear, or sense their loved one's presence. Most find these experiences very comforting.

For example, one family felt tremendous joy when a rare butterfly landed in front of them as they entered the church for their grandmother's funeral. They were astonished as "Sarah" had spent much time in futile attempts developing her garden to attract this butterfly, enduring the family's gentle teasing regarding this. Sarah's sign gave her family tremendous relief knowing that her love for them would endure. Sensory experiences of our deceased loved ones are a normal and common experience among grievers.

Contrast this with "Elena," who lost her husband, "Luis," after a long and loving marriage. In the initial session, which occurred many months after Luis died, it became clear that Elena was anxious and not doing well. She reported having nightly dreams of Luis and found these nightmares quite disturbing. Elena became sleep-deprived and was losing weight off her thin frame. She felt isolated and afraid to tell anyone what she was experiencing. Her symptoms of grief were worsening, not waning over time. Elena needed an evaluation for treatment beyond normal grief.

Complicated grief can manifest itself in the ways it does for normal grief; however, it is longer in duration and intensity. Those experiencing it may feel stuck or give up trying to cope. In extreme cases, grievers may refuse to acknowledge the death. Not acknowledging the death is not a normal reaction and requires professional help.

It's important to acknowledge that some people are so overwhelmed by the magnitude of or trauma surrounding their loss that they don't return to any sense of normalcy, becoming a shadow of their former selves.

I once worked with a woman 25 years after a traumatic accident that caused her to lose everything: her family, her job and her health. She had cut herself off even from those who stood by her, unable to forgive herself. even though the loss was accidental and unintended.  We crafted a way to address her long-standing grief, which was well entrenched after so many years. It didn't happen overnight but she was eventually able to forgive herself and a spark of life returned. She was finally able to begin letting friends back into her life again.

Perhaps you know someone who has been stuck in long-standing grief. It is never too late to seek professional help for such a loss.

The experience of grief is a wide-ranging experience impacting the whole person. Normal grief reactions vary, but most grievers can sense incremental improvements in their mood, how their body feels, and interest in previously enjoyed activities over time, although there can and often will be a revisiting of earlier grief. The grief that is not improving, the intensity of emotion, and symptoms that are not waning, can cause concern and is a reason to seek professional help.

## CHILDREN AND GRIEF

It is a sad fact that 1 in 14 children will have a parent or sibling die before they are 18.  They deal with many of the issues adults do but without the associated wisdom or life experience. Many children who have lost a parent are acutely aware of the grief of the surviving parent and go to great lengths to keep them happy.  Not surprisingly these same children grow up to be adults who put great emphasis on the importance of family, having experienced the devastation of such an early loss.

### Helping Your Child Grieve (ages 11 and under)

The best way to help your child grieve is to grieve yourself.

Children will mimic what they see and in witnessing some of your moments of grief, you are giving them permission to grieve as well.

Talk with your child as soon as possible after the death. Use the appropriate words like "death," "dead," and "died." Do not use the terms "gone," "away," or "asleep." No small child will want to go to bed after that! Using euphemisms like "Mommy is an angel now" or "God needed grandpa in Heaven" can make your child confused about what has happened and fear that God may need you in Heaven too.

Talk about the death in a simple but age-appropriate way; do not spend time on too much detail with young children. Always use the name (for example, Mary or Mom) of your deceased loved one when speaking of them. Do spend time talking with your child about your own beliefs, regarding God, and the afterlife, for example. It is okay if you have tears while you are talking with your child. Many parents fear that crying or breaking down in front of their children will frighten them. Crying is fine, but avoid sobbing, as your child may feel they must take care of you. Explain why you are sad, so they understand what is upsetting to you. It may be a relief for them to know that you feel the same way they do.

Avoiding any reaction to grief in an effort to protect the child is not recommended. Such an approach may make them wonder if you genuinely cared for the person who died. Even worse, the child may believe something is wrong with them because they are grieving and you don't appear to be.

Create opportunities for your child to ask questions: "I'll bet you have some questions about Daddy" may be all your child needs to open up. Answer your child's questions as they come. Young children will want to know who will do the practical things that the deceased loved one did for them, like prepare meals or put them to bed. Do not feel you have to have all the answers right away. But do let them know you will find some way or someone to help meet that need.

Do not be surprised if, after one of these conversations that your child asks, "Can I go and play now?" It does not mean that they do not care or do not understand what you have told them. Kids will still be kids and want to play with their friends.

Some children will let you know what they are thinking and feeling, and some will need help to open up. For those that do not, be proactive and ask them, "What are you feeling today?" Or a statement regarding your own thoughts: "I was thinking about your mommy today." Keep the questions open so a simple "yes" or "no" cannot answer them. If you share a thought of your own, also keep that simple like "I really miss her today." If you are still uncertain what a young child understands, ask them to tell their pet or favorite stuffed animal what has happened, and you will likely get the best information.

Most children, with preparation, should be encouraged to attend the viewing. Make sure to prepare children for the viewing, memorial, or funeral. Do not let your inexperience or avoidance of viewings and funerals get in the way of a valuable life lesson for your child. Let them know what they will see, that people may be crying and laughing and that you will answer any questions they have. With preparation, viewing the body will reduce fantasies of Daddy being on a fishing trip or Grandma being home in another state.

Discuss ways your child can say goodbye. I still remember painting a picture after my grandfather's death when I was 10. Many children will be grateful to paint or color pictures about their loved ones to process the loss. Finding an activity such as planting a tree or doing something as a family in your loved one's name may be meaningful. Keeping memories alive by talking about them frequently will be good for both of you.

Younger children sometimes act out their grief more than they talk about it. Typical reactions might be: fear of the dark, fear of you dying, nightmares, tearfulness, regressive behavior (sucking a thumb when they had previously stopped, for example), clinginess, irritability, bodily aches, and pains, and aggressive behavior.

Be sure to let your child's school know about the death and any concerns you have for your child. It is not unusual for grades to drop temporarily during the grieving period. Likewise, let your child know you are there for them, both now and in the future, as they have new questions and concerns.

### Helping Your Teenager Grieve

Teens who lose a parent or sibling to death are already in a time of tremendous developmental change. It's a time to establish their own identity, experience new feelings, deal with body image issues and turn their focus from their parents to their peers. Adding the loss of a parent or sibling to this critical time is devastating and can have life-long effects.

Be sure to advise your teens' school of the death so they are aware of the loss. Teens may grieve deeply but often try to hide their emotions from others to avoid feeling vulnerable. It is often easier for some to look for distractions to avoid the pain of their grief than to deal with it directly. Teen boys may especially struggle to control or hide how they feel, having been socialized to believe that crying is only for girls.

There may be times your teen acts as if nothing has happened when they actually feel broken inside. Feelings can shift rapidly, like "flipping a switch".

It's good to remember that most teens will not have a framework to think about death, other than "that's what happens to old people. " So, when a parent or a sibling or friend dies, they are not only grief stricken but often traumatized that it happens to younger people too.

Parents will do well to remember all the ways grief can affect adults and apply it to teens, who do not have the life experience or wisdom they may have. We know even as adults grieving a death is difficult and many of us seek to avoid the hard feelings of grief.

So how can you help a grieving teen?  First give them the respect of listening to their thoughts and feelings with an open heart. You can note that grief is different for each person and that you are interested in anything they have to say. You can normalize what your teen thinks and feels, understanding the wide range of normal grief responses. Just knowing what you feel is normal is a huge relief for adults and teens alike.

Respect your teens choices in grief, as long as they are healthy ones.

Guilt and regret tend to be intensified in children and teens.  Address any guilt that they are somehow responsible for the death: "If I wasn't late for school, she would not have had to drive me and would still be alive." Explain that everyone experiences some guilt or regret after the death of a loved one.  Teens are able to understand the concept of intent so reminding them that it was not their intention for their parent to die may be helpful.

Remind your teen to stick to a schedule of sleep, exercise (moving their bodies) and eating healthy foods. It's not unusual to have trouble falling asleep, or oversleeping. Likewise, they may struggle with eating less or overeating. Normalize these temporary changes.

Encourage creative expression in your teen whether it's journaling, painting, drawing, photography, poetry or music. Such an outlet may help them express what they can't do verbally.

Teens have a tendency to trust their peers over adults so it's good to ensure they have a safe peer or two who will listen. Peer support groups are good for teens who will likely listen best to peers.

It's important to know what resources are available for teens. Your school may know of local resources for grieving teens including the names of local counselors.  Contact your insurance company to find out which local counselors treat teens and if any of them specialize in grief. They may also be aware of local grief groups for teens. The National Alliance for Children's Grief will also list resources for grieving teens by state that include grief centers that offer groups. That information is listed under Chapter VII under Resources.

Let your teen know that the raw, overwhelming grief of the early months after a loss will change over time but the love they have for their deceased loved one will never go away. They will always remember, love and miss them and that is okay.

### GRIEVING AN EXPECTED DEATH

An expected death is when someone has a terminal illness without the possibility of a cure. This newer type of grief is a part of the changing landscape of grief due to improvements in medical care for those with very advanced disease. Today, life can be extended beyond what was previously possible. Steve Jobs, the genius behind Apple, who died eight years after being diagnosed with a pancreatic tumor, is one such example.

Learning to live with the ambiguity of hope while anticipating death over an unknown period is relatively new. Learning to manage the roller coaster of highs and lows as your loved one's disease process runs its course is a challenge that most of our families will be facing in the future with continuing advancements in medical research and technology.

If you are caring for such a family member, you have likely anticipated the probability of death. Your thoughts may alternate between hope for a cure and hope for a few more years of life together. You may rejoice when treatments bring an extension of good time, and yet, at the same time, you may also be waiting for the other shoe to drop, knowing that these reprieves will not last forever. Holding the tension between hope and grief can be challenging and stressful.  If you are experiencing this newer type of grief, please know that you deserve support, just as those grieving a death do.

## GRIEVING AN UNEXPECTED DEATH

Grieving the sudden traumatic death of a loved one involves all the characteristics of an expected death and much more. Such deaths can significantly lengthen the grieving process.  The following are some of the reasons grieving an unexpected death is more challenging:

- Emotions, especially sadness and depressed mood, may be heightened and longer-lasting.

- Anger may linger far longer as you deal with feelings of helplessness, guilt, rage and possibly revenge.

- If there is a trial or other legal entanglement, grief may be delayed until these matters finish. With appeals, these may take years to play out and may complicate grief.

The answer to the grievers' universal question "Why?" usually has its answer in the unknown, especially if it was a suicide or homicide. If the death was violent, you might experience secondary trauma imagining moments of terror or pain experienced by your loved one. Trauma adds an extra layer to grief and a complexity that often demands the support of professional help.

When an unexpected death occurs, there is no preparation for the griever, no time for what needs to be said, and no time to make amends. Sometimes guilt is heightened after such a death as the griever struggles through recent events to think of ways that their words or actions could have caused or prevented the death.

"I knew she was struggling; why didn't I call her earlier that morning?" cried "Al, a loving father whose daughter took her own life. After years of depression that responded well to treatment, his daughter had decided to stop her medication for unknown reasons. Al was well aware that his daughter was at serious risk, and he could not protect her from herself. Despite this, in his father's heart, he believed he should have been able to keep his daughter safe, and failing to do so, he chastised himself.

It is normal to feel a range of emotions with an unexpected death. Accept whatever you feel without judgment. In the aftermath of a sudden death, there are often unresolved relationship issues for grievers that may extend grief.

Part of mourning such a loss is finding a personal way to say all that you wish you could say to your loved one. You could do this through a letter you write to your loved one. You could also express your thoughts and feelings in a private conversation with your loved one. Some people develop a personal ritual to tell their loved one what they want them to know (remember Calvin, who sat on his wife's garden bench and spoke with her there?). Finally, some may seek professional support to attend to this important unfinished business.

Support is crucial; there are community agencies and services that may help you in this process, some of which are noted in the Resources section under Landscape Tools at the back of this book. Surround yourself with support and supplement that with professional help or grief groups that deal exclusively with your loss, if available. Look into online support specific to your loss; many grievers have found significant support online, and it is often available 24 hours a day.

### SHARED FAMILY LOSS

Many grievers are surprised to find that the place they expect to receive the most help is often unavailable.

Members of the same family grieving the loss of a mother, for example, may have very different responses to her death. It is important to remember that every relationship is different, even between a mother and her children. Differences between grieving styles and individual relationships with the deceased loved one can push families apart when supporting each other is most critical.

Accepting these differences among family members can do much to help you maintain the support you need from each other as you each learn to live with your loss.

Consider the following scenario: a daughter who lived next door to her mother, serving as a neighbor, friend, and ultimately caregiver, may struggle more with the hole left in her day-to-day life after the death than others within the family. A son who lives out of state, able to visit only occasionally, will grieve and possibly grieve deeply that distance kept them from spending the time together he would have liked. However, his day-to-day schedule of which his mother was not a part may serve as a good distraction as he moves through his grief.

There are other scenarios: the daughter who lived next door may have had the chance to repair or deepen the relationship with her mother and had opportunities to express love and thanks and ultimately to say goodbye. Though grieving her mother's death, she may also feel both peace and gratitude for having this special time with her.

The out-of-town son may have limited his visits home for various reasons, such as expense, his own family and work responsibilities, and possibly relationship issues with his mother or sister or both. Guilt over not visiting more frequently, not making peace with his mother or sister, or not being present for the death may complicate his grief.

Neither scenario is better or worse than the other; just different—and normal.

# Chapter Four

## LOCAL COLOR

*Moon Glow*

## SADNESS

Sometimes I meet concerned family or friends who are worried that a loved one is not grieving because they see no evidence of tears.

Tears may be common in grief, but they are not mandatory. Research shows that the chemical makeup of tears cried in response to a stressor, such as grief, is different than the tears cried when chopping an onion, for example. One such difference is a peptide called Leucine Enkephalin containing a natural pain killer that helps to "regulate the body back." People report feeling relief after crying so often it's referred to as "a good cry." [8]

Some research has suggested that tears denote vulnerability, something that is necessary for social connection. In this case, tears may be a way to solicit empathy and support from others, something we may sorely need in our grief. It takes a lot of energy to avoid crying, so if you feel like crying, go ahead and do so.

Some people are worried that if they allow themselves to cry, they will never stop. And it may indeed feel that way for a time. Some will cry at some point every day for a long time after a loss, and others will not. When it is time to stop crying, you will.

If you fear not being able to stop crying at work, there is something you might try. Find a private place (your car, restroom stall, empty office, for example) for privacy. Press your hand on your abdomen and take in a deep breath through your nose, inflating your belly, then expel it in a long, slow, cleansing exhalation through your mouth. Continue with this cycle until you regain calm. Crying should stop because it is physiologically impossible to cry and deep breathe at the same time.

Throughout life, there will likely continue to be times of sadness when tears come as you realize your loved one is not here to graduate high school with their class, to hold the new grandbaby, or enjoy a long dreamed of adventure with you. This sadness is normal and to be expected, as you experience the loss from the perspective of different life stages.

What if you are someone who rarely cries? Perhaps you cannot remember the last time you did. That is okay too.

Not everyone grieves primarily through their emotions. Virtually any grieving style that allows the griever to confront and not ignore grief, is healthy.

Regardless of how you grieve, it is crucial to find healthy ways to discharge grief-related stress. Dealing with stress by overindulging in food, alcohol, drugs, sex, gambling, or shopping, for example, can create problems lasting long after your loved one's death. They create rather than reduce stress.

Failure to address grief directly through healthy outlets can force it out "sideways" in illness, physical pain, addiction, and obesity, challenging your ability to cope. Unrelieved and unresolved grief only deepens over time.

## ANGER

Although many grievers do not experience anger after a loved one's death, those who do may feel overwhelmed by or uncomfortable with such feelings.

It is not uncommon, for example, to feel angry at your deceased loved one for abandoning you, even though intellectually you know that they did not choose to do so. Perhaps your anger is focused on a health care provider, health system, insurance company, or even God for allowing this to happen to your loved one. Others may feel angry in general without a clear source for their anger.

Sharing your feelings of anger with others can be awkward and embarrassing; not sharing your anger at all, however, can further isolate you. If you choose to share such feelings, only do so with those whom you trust.

Some people grow up believing anger is an unacceptable emotion. For example, many women have learned that "good" girls do not get angry, that in fact, it is "not attractive" for a woman to be angry. Some will unconsciously repress their anger to keep it at bay. Repressing anger over time can damage your health, allowing the anger to eat away at you.

Suppressing anger, on the other hand, is the deliberate redirection of anger to manage it. Examples of anger suppression techniques are: counting to ten, deep breathing, and removing yourself from then source of your anger (if that is possible). These are effective for some; for others, the energy of anger may need a safe physical discharge for the griever to feel relief.

Keeping up a pretense of being okay when you are seething inside takes a toll on your mind, body, and spirit. Physically discharging your anger on others is neither a healthy nor acceptable release of anger. Studies have shown that letting someone "have it" physically or verbally increases rather than decreases angry feelings. Dealing with anger directly through a physical outlet is often the healthiest way to discharge anger's pent-up energy.

Consider some of the healthy ways possible to release your anger, such as engaging in physical exercise. Certain games, such as pickleball, tennis, badminton, racquetball, or other games that allow you to experience the smack of a ball, can be very effective in safely discharging your anger.

Here are some suggestions that have worked for others who have found themselves stuck in their anger. Make sure you do these in private when you know you will not disturb others so you can freely yell, scream, or otherwise voice your rage.

- Beat your mattress or couch with a shoe.

- Punch a punching bag

- Kick an open paper bag around the room.

- Tear up magazines.

- Twist and wring a wet towel.

- Tightly squeeze a stress ball.

As you begin to feel your anger waning over time, you may still experience anger surges. Go back to one of the above suggestions or use whatever healthy approach has helped you in the past. Sometimes we cannot name the reason for our anger. It is essential to understand that feelings occur in response to thoughts. Allow some time to identify what thoughts are behind your anger. Sometimes anger is a cover for other emotions. Anger often happens when we feel injured, fearful, powerless, or vulnerable. Once you know what is driving your anger, you can plan to deal with the real issue.

People are often angry, for example, when a diagnosis is made far too late despite repeated trips to report the same symptoms to a health care provider. Anger can surface at the employer whose work exposed your loved one to a toxic substance and subsequent terminal illness. Feeling powerless to prevent your loved one's death, getting the insurance company to cover necessary treatments, or receiving benefits promised by an employer in a timely fashion are just a few of many ways powerlessness can induce an anger reaction.

Some grievers may find that ruminating over angry feelings encourages their anger to grow. Taking time out from worry, combined with refocusing on other activities such as list-making, playing soothing music, cooking, or other activities of interest, is helpful for some grievers.

Sometimes allowing yourself to stay angry for extended periods is a way of avoiding the pain of grief. Anger can give us a sense of control when it seems as if we have no control over anything else. It can also provide the illusion that your righteous anger is what connects you to your loved one, so you allow it to continue in an attempt to keep the bond secure.

**FEAR**

Fear can rear its ugly head when we feel the most vulnerable, such as a time of grief.  Many grievers experience the fear of loneliness, fear of spending the rest of one's life alone, fear of the future, or even the fear of death itself. Fear of the unknown, of what the rest of life will be like, of how you will manage, can be the most overwhelming fear of all.

Financial concerns can ramp up fear, especially if it requires significant life changes for survivors. Being left without life insurance or other planning in place or needing to re-enter the workplace again (or for the first time) are two examples of many fears one can experience. If you feel paralyzed by fear or your fears are undiminished even months later, talking with a mental health professional may be of benefit to you.

**UNFORGIVENESS**

Imagine you are traveling on foot in a place where the terrain is unfamiliar. You have brought a few things with you from your former life to give you comfort and help you on your journey, but you find that your ability to move forward seems hampered by the weight of your backpack. It seems heavier and heavier with each step, slowing your pace and making movement difficult. Curious, you set the backpack down to peek inside. To your dismay, you find a heavy rock inside. No wonder it was so hard to move forward!

Trying to move forward after the death of someone you have not forgiven can be the rock that slows you down and creates a burden.

Being unforgiving, like carrying a heavy rock in your backpack, can be debilitating, affecting you emotionally, physically, and spiritually. Someone you trusted may have hurt you deeply, taken advantage of you, or in some way harmed you or someone you love. Anger, perhaps even rage, that you placed your trust in someone who proved untrustworthy might come in waves. "How could she do this to me?" Sometimes reasons remain a mystery. Even knowing the answer may not be enough to move on from this stuck position.

Occasionally, a griever may unexpectedly discover a hidden part of their loved one's life after the death. It could be an affair or owing a large debt, for example, among many other possibilities. Discovering something your loved one hid from you may complicate grief as you attempt to negotiate your disbelief and anger at this betrayal. In such circumstances, talking with a mental health professional is strongly encouraged.

Once you manage your anger, please consider forgiveness. Forgiveness is one of the most misunderstood concepts on the planet. Here is what it is not:

- It is not condoning what someone did to you; harming you or someone you love is not okay!

- It does not necessarily mean that you feel forgiving. If we waited until we felt like forgiving someone, forgiveness would rarely happen.

- It does not mean you wave a magic wand and say, "I forgive you," and feel no more anger.

Unfortunately, so many people go to their graves, withholding forgiveness, never grasping that their refusal to forgive has taken them prisoner. We all can choose how to move forward and conduct ourselves even when nothing else is in our control. We can choose to stop our feelings from holding us hostage any longer.

Forgiveness is a process involving an act of the will. Like anything worthwhile, it takes time. People who have hurt you deeply sometimes do not realize, do not understand, or possibly do not care what they have done. When you live in an anger or revenge state, your life revolves around the other person, and your focus is a point in time that has passed. The process of forgiveness allows you to remove yourself from the victim orbit, come fully into the present, and move forward in freedom.

I am not suggesting that you not feel whatever feelings you have. On the contrary, you have to name, acknowledge, and experience what you feel first to let it go. Forgiveness is not saying that what happened to you is acceptable.

At some point, however, when you tire of carrying this burden, you might ask yourself the following:

"How long do I want to be held hostage to these feelings?"

"How would I prefer to feel?"

"What am I not doing now that would be good for my family and other relationships if I forgive?"

"What could I be doing, and how would I be feeling right now if I were free of this burden?"

Forgiveness is often more comfortable if we have seen it modeled in our original family. However, you may not have witnessed forgiveness in your home.

There are many amazing stories online that truly illustrate the power of forgiveness. One of the most remarkable is that of Rais Bhuiyan, a young Bangladeshi man living in New York shortly after the terrorist attacks on 9/11/2001. He almost didn't survive being shot in the face by a white supremacist named Mark Anthony Stroman, who was out for revenge due to the attacks. Stroman was convicted and placed on death row.  It took a long time for Bhuiyan to recover, including multiple surgeries. Ultimately, he still lost his sight in one eye. Once Bhuiyan recovered, he decided to keep his promise that, should he survive, he would do more for others. He began an active attempt to overturn Stroman's death penalty.

The day of execution came, and the last-ditch effort in federal court to stay the execution, failed. That day Bhuiyan and Stroman spoke by phone for the first and only time. "I forgive you, and I do not hate you," Bhuiyan said. Stroman responded, "Thank you from my heart! I love you, bro. You touched my heart. I would have never expected this." Bhuiyan replied: "You touched mine, too." [9]

Bhuiyan went onto establish a nonprofit group entitled World Without Hate with the mission of "breaking the cycle of hate and violence through empathy and storytelling". Check chapter VII: Landscape Tools. You will find the URL for the World without Hate website and one for The Forgiveness Project with inspiring true stories of forgiveness by survivors and their families from around the world.

## GUILT

Some grievers fall into the routine of mental  flogging called "woulda, coulda, shoulda." Some may feel guilty for the loss: "if only I had not asked him to go to the store for me, he would not have died" or "If only I had taken her to the doctor earlier, she would still be here." These and other similar thoughts may take up residence in your mind. Sometimes there may be an element of truth to these ruminations, and sometimes it is entirely out of our control, as death often is.

We are often our last holdout. Our mercy may flow like a river to others, but we may build a steep and slippery embankment for ourselves.

What do we gain by remaining trapped in this way? Not forgiving myself allows me to continue to believe perfection is attainable. Then I can punish myself as retaliation for being imperfect.

Some of us grew up in families where survival meant doing things as perfectly as possible to avoid conflict or drawing the anger of an abusive caregiver. It may have worked and kept us safe, at least some of the time when we were children. But to be a healthy adult, chronic guilt related to perfectionism, does not serve us well at all.

Not forgiving yourself implies that you hold a double standard—one for others and a higher one for yourself. You may have indeed been held to such high standards in the past by parents, teachers, friends, and others. But now you know better; now the only one holding you hostage is—you.

Being only human, we are sure to fall short at times. Self-forgiveness is an act of humility. Forgiving oneself reduces depression and can increase our energy to be more creative, loving, and free. In the end, forgiveness, whether for yourself or another, is freeing.  Sometimes if guilt is prolonged, it allows us to avoid the other painful emotions of grief.

If your guilt continues to cause you anxiety, or if it continues undiminished months after the death, talking with a mental health professional is highly recommended.

**SPIRITUAL PAIN**

You may feel distant from your faith at a time you need it most.

You may not want to attend religious services or return to the site of the funeral. Or you may feel the faith you had previously crumble in your anger at God for allowing this to happen to your loved one and you. These are normal responses to loss that may last for many months and sometimes much longer. Most people who experience these feelings eventually come back to their faith, although the breach may be permanent for some.

If you have spiritual questions or feel stuck in your anger, unforgiveness, or guilt, consider speaking with someone from your faith community. It does not necessarily have to be the priest, minister, or rabbi, but it should be someone you trust not to judge your doubts and fears, as well as someone that respects your grief.

Spiritual direction is an option to consider. It allows someone (a trained Spiritual Director) to accompany you as a caring witness in your lived experience with God or your Higher Power. Spiritual Directors receive professional training to help you discern where God or your Higher Power is touching your life directly or indirectly. To consider the availability of Spiritual Direction in your area, check with your faith community or search online for "spiritual directors near me."

On the other hand, you may feel more convicted than ever by your faith. Your relationship with God may be a source of tenderness and compassion as you travel the rocky terrain of grief, allowing you to experience a deepening and widening of your faith in a way you could not anticipate. You may sense the presence of God in a way you have never experienced previously.

Whether we rail at the heavens or seek much-needed solace in our spirituality, grief challenges us to define ourselves at this most basic and sacred level. A healthy spirituality does not protect you from loss; instead, it allows you to embrace and fully experience it. A healthy spirituality can help you accept what cannot be changed and, ultimately, help you find peace.

Many faith communities recognize the need to respond with compassion to their grieving members and have developed grief support groups. Some have established entire ministries that offer trained volunteer listeners and tangible support through home-delivered meals and other services. If you belong to such a community, consider asking for help. After all, that is why it is there.

## LAUGHTER

Some people believe laughter has no role in grief. There certainly isn't anything inherently humorous about the death of a loved one. And yet, sometimes, the ironies of our circumstances, little details that would usually pass unnoticed, or remembrances of humorous times with our loved ones can provide welcome relief in grief, if only for a moment.

It happened at my father's rosary service during his visitation the night before his funeral. At the end of the service, the organist began to play the Irish song my father had requested: Galway Bay. It was surprising as we had never heard our father sing or mention this song before, but we wanted to honor his request.

My brother, seated next to our mother, seemed overcome with emotion, his face covered by his hand. I was in a fog, caring for my young children and my anticipation of the next day, and did not listen to the music. I did notice others looking perplexed and a couple of people smirking, which caught me off guard. What could possibly be funny?

As soon as the music stopped, my sister's friend turned to her with a smile and said, "I didn't know your Dad's favorite song was the Oscar Meyer Weiner song!". My brother immediately recognized the commercial tune and covered his face with his hand attempting to suppress his laughter. Those in attendance may not have heard Galway Bay before, but they definitely knew the familiar tune from TV commercials.

None of us would put it past our father to do something like this as a joke. He loved to joke around and laughed just as hard when the joke was on him. We agreed he had likely heard the song somewhere once, liked it, and impulsively left a note to have it played at his service. Depending on the cadence of how one played the music, it might have sounded different. But played briskly by the funeral home organist, it evoked images of hotdogs and summertime.

There seems to be a fine line between tears and laughter. It makes sense as both may:

- Be healing.

- Help our immune system and reduce stress.

- Help us process our loss.

Even in grief, there are times when laughter may come unexpectedly. If you find yourself laughing, go ahead and laugh: it's good for you.

# Chapter Five

---

# VARIATIONS in the LANDSCAPE

*Arcadia Overlook*

## GRIEVING the DEATH of a CHILD

The death of a child at any age is the most devastating of life experiences.

Not only the child is mourned but their lost potential, our dreams for them, and their future. The opportunity to make new memories with them is gone forever. Grieving parents need a way to honor the gift of their child's life. A child's death is out of the natural order of things; no one expects their child to pre-decease them. The trauma of such a loss often deepens and lengthens the grieving process.

Grieving parents often find the most solace in the company of other grieving parents. Many communities have grief centers, hospices, or church-run grief group support to help parents and sometimes siblings after a child dies.

Providing connection with other parents who have "been there" is the mission of Compassionate Friends who seek to support parents whose child has died at any age by any means, as well as their families. They have nearly 600 chapters in the United States, which offer friendship, understanding, and hope. See Resources under Chapter VII: Landscape Tools at the back of the book for more information on Compassionate Friends.

Keeping a child's memory alive through annual fundraisers is one way some parents memorialize their children. Some have noted that developing a webpage (some of which are free) in honor of their child gave them tremendous satisfaction.

If you have lost a child to death, please check out the resources noted on the Resources pages in Chapter VII Landscape Tools. Also check with your health care provider and insurance company for resources as well.

## HIDDEN GRIEF

Our culture determines who has the legitimate right to grieve and receive support for a specific loss, as well as what losses are legitimate to grieve. Some of life's most difficult losses involve hidden grief. Because it is not recognized, many people find themselves isolated and without support.

Some don't even recognize that what they are feeling is grief. These hidden losses are called "disenfranchised" or hidden loss: being deprived of the right to grieve. Here are some typical comments expressed regarding some common disenfranchised losses:

- Death of an ex-spouse: "Why would you grieve? You divorced him, didn't you? "

- Death of a pet: "Can you believe how she is behaving? It was just a cat !"

- Financial losses/foreclosure: "I don't feel sorry for you; you did it to yourself. "'

- Job loss/forced retirement: "Why so sad? Now you can do what you have never had time for."

Here is one example of such a loss. A young man named "Nate" experienced significant grief when his elderly neighbor "Miguel" died. No one understood why this had such a profound impact on him. Miguel had functioned as a father figure to Nate, and so he grieved Miguel as he would a father. He mourned his death harder than he had the death of his own, often absent, father. It was hard enough to be grieving and even harder when others were perplexed as to why he was so upset over the death of someone who was "just a neighbor. "

If you are grieving a hidden loss, it is essential to know that the problem lies with the culture, not with you. You have a right to grieve and receive the support that you need. But finding such support may be tricky. Seek support first among those with whom you already have trusting relationships. Always choose carefully with whom you share your loss. If no one you know can fill this role, I encourage you to seek professional help.

### DEATH AFTER a PAINFUL or COMPLICATED RELATIONSHIP

Sometimes death signifies an end to a difficult or painful relationship. The ambiguity in such a loss—to grieve while experiencing relief at the end of a relationship with an addict, abuser, someone who betrayed you, or who had a secret life, can be painful and isolating.

It is difficult in our culture to hold two contradictory ideas in mind at the same time. Yet, these contradictions occur to a greater or lesser extent in many relationships. It is not uncommon, for example, to love someone who has an addiction that casts an enormous shadow over the relationship. These and other confounding issues often can and do coexist.

In the month I was to finish graduate school, a fellow student, pregnant and separated from her husband, got a call advising her that he was killed in a car accident on the way to work. When I expressed my sadness to another student, he said, "Well, it isn't like they were going to get back together or anything! " As if that somehow made her grief less legitimate or lighter. Of course, now there would be no possibility to reconcile, to enjoy parenthood together, to make amends, or at least to end the relationship with some care and dignity. Such a loss can greatly complicate grief.

If you loved someone with whom you could not enjoy the relationship you longed for or if aspects of the relationship went unfulfilled, it is helpful to acknowledge and grieve these losses. As you lean into the pain of your unfulfilled dream, notice what bubbles up for you: Sadness? Anger? Fear? Relief?

Ideally, you can talk this through with someone you trust. Unfortunately for many, talking about these losses feels too embarrassing or shameful.

If you have experienced such a death, there is no need to suffer in silence. You deserve the support of those who will listen without judgment. A mental health professional can help you create a safe place to share your story, mourn, and receive the support you need.

## DEATH in a PANDEMIC

We have just finished 2 years of what seems like unending loss and grief due to the Covid-19 pandemic. We have experienced quarantine, people dying alone, shutdowns, job loss, homelessness, and a whole new kind of grief.

Hospitalized people dying of the virus usually died alone or with the caring touch of a compassionate health care provider. Their grief-stricken families experienced trauma in being robbed of the ability to extend the loving care and presence that they ached to offer. This traumatic loss will likely complicate grief and reverberate within families for many years and possibly generations to come.

For frontline workers in healthcare, grief will likely be delayed, and only surface after the crisis is truly over. Only then will they be able to contemplate and feel the magnitude of the toll on themselves and the sacrifice they have made. This delay can also complicate grief and extend well beyond what is normal.

Those of us who did not experience the death of a loved one may also be traumatized watching this pandemic play out on TV. We witnessed families where only the children survived, and families that had an entire generation wiped out. We witnessed the death of young people who had their entire lives ahead of them.

These are just a few examples of what may cause secondary trauma in those of us who watched helplessly.

The pandemic has created a tremendous need for grief therapy and support in the coming years.

As the pandemic goes on through variants, it is good to remember what we can still do to honor our loved ones. If it is possible to hold an in person memorial service that you were unable to do earlier, go ahead and schedule it. Allowing people to support you, provide stories you may not have heard and in general, acknowledge the importance of your loved one's life, is part of your healing. Don't think that the passage of time means it's too late to do this. It's okay to do now, what you were unable to do earlier.

You may want to do something special in your home to remember your loved one. Some grievers have done "altars" or a sacred spot in their home where they keep pictures, mementos, and other items that remind them of their loved one and continued connection. You may light a candle there in the evening or on special occasions. Perhaps you will have a vase of flowers there to honor them. Having something you design to honor your loved one may be healing after so much has been out of your control.

Continue to stay in contact with those close to you virtually if you are unable to get out. Whether by phone or Zoom, don't underestimate the power of these contacts to help you in your grief.

Now and for the foreseeable future, virtual therapy sessions are available for those who are unable or unwilling to leave their home at this time. Contact your insurance company to see who may be available to do such sessions. Also check out the Psychology Today's Find–a-Therapist section on its website. They usually will note if they are offering such sessions.

## THE DEATH of a PET

Most of us have had a beloved pet and then grieved its inevitable death. As any animal lover knows, losing a pet can be just as devastating—and sometimes more devastating—than the death of a family member. Pet loss falls into the category of hidden or disenfranchised loss: loss that is not socially recognized as appropriate to mourn. Pet lovers know better: our pets are family members too.

Although bereavement leave for pet owners is not recognized, most workplaces have had to deal with this. I remember my friend "Karla", who happily resided with her pets and kept everyone in her workplace entertained with stories of their endearing quirks and antics. It was no surprise when she was unable to work after the death of her very aged dog. Karla only took off a couple of days, and it took everything she had to return to work even then. But the death of her furry family member left a huge void.

Some people believe that grieving for a pet is somehow odd. Yet, for many people, a pet is the only living thing that has ever loved them unconditionally. These are intelligent, capable people who have found that one of their most faithful companions had four legs (or fins, feathers, etc.)

A pet serves so many needs, and these needs must be identified and mourned. Research shows that among the many benefits pets provide is a reduction in our stress level, lowering our blood pressure and cholesterol, and an overall enhancement of our quality of life. Is it any wonder that people with pets live longer?

Some funeral homes and hospices now offer grief groups for pet owners because they recognize the need for support. Do not apologize for your grief; every death, including those of our pets, requires and deserves time to grieve. If you have endured the death of your pet, find a sympathetic pet owner who will listen or locate a grief support group for pet owners.

As a psychotherapist, I have worked with people who did not have anyone who understood the impact that their pets' death had on their lives. Seek professional help if you need it.

### RETURNING to WORK AFTER the DEATH of a LOVED ONE

Marla felt some anxiety about returning to work after her husband's death. Ultimately she realized that Coming back to work offered her something she could not get anywhere else: routine, structure, and distraction. Working was helpful—for a while. Over time, what was initially comforting to her became something to dread. She looked so good when she initially returned that it lulled her boss and others into thinking that she was back to work as usual. When her coworkers saw what a good adjustment she was making, they didn't realize that her grief was still raw after watching her beloved die over the course of two years. Things started to unravel for Marla. When she began missing essential details in her work, coming late to meetings, and missing a necessary appointment—the antithesis of her former self—others took notice. Marla was so convincing about separating her grief from her work that her boss could not understand the change. When Marla resigned, he felt both confusion—and relief.

This scenario gets played out over and over again in workplaces every year. Lives often play out at work: struggles with teenagers, separations and divorces, hot flashes, and deaths of loved ones are all witnessed by our work colleagues. The old belief about keeping your personal life at home often does not work.

No one understands until they have lost a loved one, how little things can trigger your grief unexpectedly. If supervisors do not know what to expect when a grieving employee returns to work, they may perceive a competent but grieving employee as a problematic employee.

Grievers should consider making a plan to handle grief attacks on the job before returning to work. Grief attacks are when emotions or thoughts of your loved one come unbidden and catch you off guard. You were feeling well, and then you hear your loved one's favorite song playing or listen to plans coworkers are making for the weekend, for example, and are reminded that you will no longer be making such plans with your loved one. Or you think of something that you want to share with your loved one, and you pull up your email to contact them only to remember the reality of the death. Suddenly you are very much in touch with your wrenching sense of loss.

Consider your options: where can you find ten minutes to pull yourself together if you have a grief attack? Is there a vacant office available? Even going out to your car or walking around the block (if that is a possibility) can be your plan. Planning is essential: it is not a matter of if such episodes will occur, but when. You should anticipate these as a normal part of grieving.

Before you return to work, here are a few other things to consider in light of your changed circumstances:

- Do you need to locate childcare or eldercare now?

- Is it better for you initially to phase back into work on a reduced schedule or return part-time?

- Will you need help with aspects of your work that require significant attention to detail? (Remember that the inability to concentrate is the hallmark of grief).

- What do you need your coworkers to know before you return?

For example, do you want to talk about your loss at work, or do you prefer not to? Your supervisor or HR professional can convey your wishes to your coworkers before you return to work. Your colleagues will be relieved to know your wishes and make it less likely you will have to deal with each concerned colleague who approaches you.

Make an appointment with your supervisor or Human Resources (or both) to discuss these and other concerns you may have in returning to work. Agree to meet regularly to evaluate how you are doing and tweak whatever plan is in place as your circumstances and needs change. Do not apologize for your grief, but do reassure them of your continued loyalty and commitment to the company.

### MANAGING HOLIDAY GRIEF

Anticipating the holidays after the death of a loved one is something that may fill you with dread.

Should you do what you have always done? Will altering traditions make things easier? There is no one size fits all answer. The most important thing to remember is to anticipate these challenging times and create a plan that works for you. Failing to make contingency plans for holidays and other important dates is planning to fail, as many grievers have learned the hard way.

Everyone is different. If you are uncertain of what you want to do, let family and friends who expect you to attend their gatherings know that you will likely make that decision on the day of the gathering when you know how you feel.

If you wake up and feel okay—then go; if you wake up and realize you need to care for yourself by staying away from the festivities, plan something that is not so full of the expectation to be joyful. If you do attend a function, let your hosts know beforehand that you may leave early if you need to.

It is possible to find ways to celebrate by making some adjustments in expectations for yourself and the expectations others may have for you. Sometimes we get stuck in the past when baking cookies for days, and hosting the annual neighborhood party for 100 was an expected part of the celebration. You do not have to do the same things you have always done year after year, especially when things have changed so drastically for you.

Are you the only one who can do those necessary holiday traditions? Who else could perform these functions this year? Is there anything on the list you are looking forward to doing?

Make one list for the things you must do that you will need help with and another for those things you want to do. At this point, friends and family who have made broad offers to do anything you need can help. For example, if you have young children at home, having a tree and gifts may be very important; let your friends help arrange to complete these and other items on your must-do list. Allowing others to help you takes humility but gives those helping you something to do to show you how much they care—let them! It benefits you both.

Remembering your loved one in some meaningful way during the season may bring comfort. Here are a few suggestions:

- Leave your loved one's seat empty at the holiday dinner table the first year as a reminder of your continued love and connection.

- Share cherished memories over a meal.

- Consider remembering gifts that your loved one left you, such as a sense of humor, compassion, or curiosity. Pick one each day of the holiday season and reflect on its meaning for you.

- Buy a gift that reflects your loved one's interest and choose someone different to gift it to every year.

- Donate to your loved one's favorite charity in their name.

My own parents loved celebrating holidays and went to great lengths to make them fun for us. Celebrating the holidays after their deaths felt hollow in their absence. I realized I needed to find a way to bring my parents into the celebration.

I decided to set up a double frame with their pictures setting a candle in front of it. I light the candle each night at dusk during the holidays. In this way I am honoring the people who taught me how to celebrate and letting others know my parents are still a part of my celebration.

Finally, it is vital to take special care to eat, exercise, and get enough rest. Find at least one thing, however small, that you can be grateful for each day. Stay true to your spiritual practices to heal your grieving heart. Above all, be kind and treat yourself with tenderness and care.

## PLANNING for ANNIVERSARIES and SPECIAL DATES

I remember a client named "Zain," who did well in the first year after his wife, "Francie," died in a car accident. After a short bereavement leave, he returned to work only to have his job transferred to another division, which he handled with grace.

He planned and took a long-anticipated trip with a friend, something Francie never wanted to do. He took up playing the guitar, another long-held dream, taking lessons, and diligently practicing every day. He did well, weathering most of the firsts of that initial year without Francie.

Until the anniversary of her death, that is. He had spent the day alone and, in the evening, called a close friend and said, "I can't take this anymore; I have reached my limit." The friend was frightened enough to call the police, who picked him up and took him to the hospital, where he was admitted to the psychiatric unit. He felt mortified and humiliated. He had no intention of killing himself, but his veiled threat was something his frightened friend could not ignore.

When we began working together, one of Zain's first goals was to make a plan for the hard days that would include at least one other person since he believed his isolation contributed to his depressed mood on the anniversary.

After considering several options, he picked one that appealed to him that would include a friend and a close relative. He then talked with both of them about committing to being with him on his upcoming wedding anniversary, which they readily agreed to do.

It was a simple plan: he wanted to take flowers and visit the grave alone to honor his wife. Then he would join his friend and relative, and they would go out to dinner with a couple of other close friends who also loved Francie and reminisce over a good meal.

Thinking it might be difficult for Zain if he felt tearful at a restaurant, his relative offered to host the dinner at her own home, preparing his favorite meal. The dinner was low-key, and they all enjoyed not only moments of sadness but much laughter as well, recalling Francis's playful personality. When Zain lay down to sleep that night, he felt he had honored Francie in the way she deserved and knew that her memory would not be forgotten by those who loved her.

It is critically important to plan for anniversaries, birthdays, and any other dates you anticipate as hard just as you do with holidays. Hoping things will go well on their own rarely works. Planning will also make it harder for well-meaning others to plan that day for you. While their intentions may be good, their plan may not address your needs. Only you can say what those needs are.

# Chapter Six

# UNCHARTED TERRITORY

*Uncharted Territory*

**LIVING IN-BETWEEN**

At some point as you grieve, you will likely wonder, "Who am I now?"

Grief creates a crisis of identity. You still retain your life's experiences, your memories, and your gifts. However, in losing your loved one and all the secondary losses that follow, you may realize a need to explore who you are without them.

You may find that the deep grief you have experienced has given way to an in-between state where you no longer belong to the past but are not yet into your future. What made sense does not fit anymore; what you built your life on is gone, done. Being in between may feel like you are stuck, which can be both alarming and distressing. You may be surprised to know that it is likely you are on the edge of significant change.

Being in-between is unsettling; we live neither in the past nor do we have a clear future. This place of neither dark nor light, of being between history and mystery, can leave some of us grasping for some source of comfort, even if it was not or is not good for us.

It may help to remember that this in-between place is where we may need to be, for a time. We continue to grieve what once was, to prepare to move on to something different. We may need to let go of our former hopes and dreams with our loved ones to make room for newer ones, perhaps ones we cannot yet even imagine. Sometimes this in-between space is so frightening for grievers they begin to fill it with things and people who are simply space-fillers.

It is normal and natural to want to find your equilibrium, to find some comfort, to feel a sense of control, or to feel like you have some things in your life which are certain.

This in-between place is a normal and necessary place to be when we are in transition. It is not a mistake; it is not an error. We are right where we need to be. Fighting it, trying too quickly to replace what was, robs us of the opportunity to let go of what was, so we can grow into what will be, what we cannot yet imagine.

Although death may have changed some of the roles we've played and forever changed the way we live, we must remember that we are not leaving ourselves as we leave the past. We bring with us all we've become through the relationship with our loved ones. Everything we are, including gifts received from our loved ones, comes with us.

Many times, when grievers struggle to make decisions on their own, I ask them what their loved one would have advised. They immediately know what that is. Sometimes the loved one would have made them laugh to lighten their mood; other times, they may have reassured them that they were making the right decision. And still, other times, they might have provided a viewpoint they had not previously considered. That humor, that reassurance, that wisdom remains within us and is available any time.

Some upscale restaurants bring sorbet to cleanse the palate between two very different courses. Eating the sorbet helps to shift from one taste and texture to another, to be able to taste and enjoy the next course. And so it is with grief: give yourself the gift of time spent in this in-between space so when you are ready, you can move into and enjoy your future.

## SELF-ASSESSMENT

At some point in the months following the death, and again after the one-year anniversary of the death has passed, it is good to take stock of how you are faring with your grief.

How will you evaluate this? Although some experts recommend seeing a grief specialist if undiminished intense grieving is still present at the one-year mark, this may be premature. At one year, you may experience an anniversary reaction, a common and normal revisiting of some of the intensity of your initial grief.

An anniversary reaction can create a false sense of emergency, a sense that you have not been doing as well as you thought you were. You will likely recycle through many of your previous feelings and periodically do so beyond that first anniversary. Be mindful of your feelings, acknowledging them without judgment. There is nothing else to be done because feelings will pass. Not that you have finished grieving; that may still go on. But your early baby steps in grief may have turned into a more sure-footed walk.

Ask yourself the following question: "Am I doing better than I was six months ago? A year ago?" Think of change in terms of small steps, not leaps. Have you returned to some of the things in life you previously enjoyed, such as spending time with friends or watching your grandchildren? If you feel you are coming to life again, that is a good indication that you are not "stuck" in grief. Please remember that the manner of death, if sudden or violent, adds trauma to the mix and can make grieving more difficult and longer-lasting.

Those whom we have loved dearly can never be forgotten or replaced. As you move through grief, the landscape changes, and you may find:

- You are having more good days than bad days.

- Your memories of your loved one focus more on what you loved and treasured about them and less on the death.

- You experience more prolonged periods when you are not thinking of your loved one.

- Your quality of sleep improves.

- Your energy increases.

- You find your mind clearing and your ability to concentrate is improved and longer-lasting.

- You are thinking more about the future and are trying new experiences.

- You are laughing again, and your sadness is less frequent and intense.

It is crucial to know that there may be times in the future that you experience occasional grief attacks, perhaps around holidays, anniversaries, birthdays, or other significant events. Grief attacks are normal and do not mean you are still in intense mourning or that you have done anything wrong.

Loving someone lasts a lifetime. As you move forward, there will be some sunny days, some cloudy days, and some days of each mixed with occasional bouts of grief. These bouts of grief do not contradict the fact that you are healing. These mixed times coexist in most lives touched by loss.

## LIVING with INTENTION

As you heal and come to feel more whole, consider what you can do today to honor, improve or repair your existing relationships with family and friends.

One lesson often learned in grief is this: do not postpone telling loved ones what you want them to know today. If you knew your life was limited to a week, what is left undone or unfinished in your life? Our lives are rarely in perfect order when we die; however, we can still do what we can do if we are alive today. What would you do differently, if anything? What would you stop doing? What would you want to try? Who needs a call from you?

What and who came to mind for you? What stops you from finishing a vital life task, taking more time with family and friends, or making amends? If you are too shy or intimidated to speak your feelings, write your feelings and thoughts in an email or letter.

Death has a way of reminding us that we truly have only the present moment. What you do with today while you have it may determine whether you have regrets after someone you love dies. Next to the grief associated with death is the grief of those who have lost but not learned. Push through complacency and do what you can do now for those you love.

Consider also what you can do to improve the ability of the next generation in your family to grieve in healthy ways.

Hopefully, you will find some teachable moments to share with your family what you have done to manage your grief. They need not do it your way; they will navigate their inner landscape of grief in their own way. Knowing that you allowed yourself to grieve and came through it will positively affect your children and grandchildren.

Having such conversations can significantly improve the health and well-being of family you will never even meet. Sharing your grief experience is a beautiful gift and legacy to your current and future family. If some are currently unwilling to discuss this, consider writing your thoughts down. You could write a letter or an ethical will to convey your thoughts.. An ethical will is a document where one shares one's life lessons and wisdom with those who come after them. They may not be interested now, but at some point, this will be important, helpful, and treasured information. If you do not teach them, how will they learn?

## OPENING to POSSIBILITIES in the CHANGING LANDSCAPE

It is human nature to seek the known, to seek stasis in life. Ironically, it is life's nature to be unpredictable and inconsistent. The course you have charted can no longer get you where you planned to go. Many of us only look to cross the ocean of unknown when we are forced to do so. Sometimes courage to lose sight of our shore is the reluctant movement of fear, knowing that we cannot stay where we are because what we had no longer exists.

That is okay. We may be stepping out of our comfort zone for the very first time. Doing so may take us places we cannot yet imagine. Change (not death) can be a good thing. In opening ourselves to a changing landscape, we open ourselves to growth and wisdom and a world of possibilities. Often it is only in hindsight that we can say, "This is not what I wanted or planned, but now I know I can handle anything."

Be open to possibilities rather than trying to make the perfect plan for your life. Some things may have to be done quickly due to financial, legal, or unforeseen circumstances. As unbelievable as it sounds, opportunities may pop up when you are ready as you heal and move forward into your future.

Remember that as long as you are breathing, you can learn to do new things and to do old things in new ways. As you face your ocean of unknown, you might not have a boat to sail in, but you can still learn to swim if you choose to.

## A FINAL REQUEST

I have a request to make.

Only you know what terrain you have covered and what your grief travels have cost you. In walking through your grief to a place of healing, there is something that you may be uniquely qualified to offer, perhaps something someone will only get from you.

That something is this: be that loving witness providing support for those who enter the landscape of grief after you. You can provide this for those you know, and some of you may provide this for those you have yet to meet, perhaps as a trained volunteer for your local hospice or grief center.

Maybe, like me, you recall times when you missed or avoided the opportunity to be present for another griever, believing you had nothing to offer. Now we know better. We already have all we need to be present to someone who is hurting; our presence is sufficient.

It is one of life's ironies that when we give someone else our time and supportive presence in grief, we open ourselves to the healing of our own hurts. Being present for someone else may change their life—as well as your own. Offering your time and presence may make all the difference in the world to someone who would receive no support except what you are willing to give.

The late spiritual writer Henri Nouwen perhaps described it best:

> "The friend who can be silent with us in a moment of despair or confusion, who can stay with us in an hour of grief and bereavement, who can tolerate not knowing, not curing, not healing, and face with us the reality of our powerlessness, that is a friend who cares." [10]

Please consider being that loving presence, the friend who stays and does not turn away, as someone else enters their landscape of grief.

## THE END

# Chapter Seven

## LANDSCAPE TOOLS

*Pamona Park*

## JOURNAL PROMPTS

Use these questions to help you journal about your grief experience. Please note that these are not questions to be answered only once. Your answers may change over time, as you age, and as you have new experiences that shed light on your grief. If any of these questions do not pertain to you or your experience, skip them and move on to those that do.

- In what way have you spent time with your grief, either alone or with others? Are you avoiding the hard feelings of grief?

- How do you handle the stress of your grief? What works? What doesn't work?

- If crying has been part of your mourning, what brings tears to your eyes most frequently? When and where do you cry? Write about the impact that tears have had on your grief and any benefits/deficits you have found as a result.

- Identify any people or institutions with whom you are angry. Write a letter to each person or institution letting them know what they have or haven't done and how it has affected you and your loved one. For this exercise, *do not mail this letter*. Read them aloud as if you are reading to the person/institution with whom you are angry. Then burn them and let your anger go with the rising smoke.

- Do you harbor feelings of guilt? Write down any that come to mind in as much detail as possible. Ask yourself the following: Did I really have complete power to cause/prevent what happened? Did I truly intend to harm my loved one? Whom else (if anyone) may bear some of the responsibility? What will it take for me to let this go?

• How have your personal beliefs been affected by grief? What about your faith do you find most comforting? What about your faith have you found unhelpful? Who or what feeds your spirit now? With whom can you share your feelings about your faith?

• Spend time thinking about your hopes and dreams for your relationship. Name and write the fulfillment of each hope or dream and what that means to you. Then name and write down each unfulfilled hope or dream and what that means to you.

• If the relationship was difficult or complicated, what were the most challenging aspects of the relationship? If you feel what seems to be conflicting emotions, write those down as well, knowing that all are acceptable.

• Since the death, what about your life has permanently changed? Write down all the changes you've had to make.

• Since the death, what about your life has stayed the same? Write down everything that comes to mind.

• Think about all the special roles your loved one played in your life. Give these roles names that are meaningful to you (my 'rock', my confidant, my best friend, etc.) Please commit to journal about the importance of these roles and how your loved one fulfilled them.

• What has been the hardest role to lose? What have you done to fill some of these roles and to carry out necessary responsibilities? Share this with a trusted person who will listen and not judge. If you don't have someone to share this with, you may find that reading this aloud to yourself may be helpful.

• What do you need the most practical help or support with now? Identify those needs putting them in order of priority. Whom will you contact to arrange to meet these needs? What do you need to do to tackle these? If this seems overwhelming, who can act as your personal contractor to help you arrange for others to meet the practical needs you must handle immediately?

• What needs will not be met due to the death of your loved one?  Someone to listen to you, to "have your back," to support you as a parent?  If what you had was so unique some needs may go unmet. Note these also and write what these losses mean to you.

• What have you done to avoid the pain of grief? Is there a particular emotion you've been avoiding?  Do you try to avoid grief by becoming overly   involved with work, food, alcohol, drugs, or a new relationship? What would help you experience that emotion?   If you've avoided your grief, what is one small thing you can do beginning today that could help change that?  Who can you tell about your plan to encourage you to be accountable?

• What thoughts, feelings, and behaviors are you experiencing now?  Write it all down. Pick one area you would like to improve. Write these down and commit to doing them.

• Write down some of the significant changes you've made previously; how did you cope through each of those changes? What worked, what didn't work or what was harmful? What was missing for you, anything?

• Do you need a better support system? Do you need to beef up your self-care?  Pick an area for improvement, and choose one small step you can take today toward strengthening that area.

• Pick the myth of grief that has been most difficult for you.  How have you been dealing with the issue up until now?  Moving forward, how would you like to handle this issue? What steps do you need to take to deal with this? Write these down and commit to doing them.

• Where are you in terms of accepting your loss? What has helped you in this process? What has hindered this process for you? Are there times when you're more accepting of your current situation? What is different at those times that allows you greater acceptance?

• If acceptance has been a struggle for you, what is one step that can help you with this? Write it down and commit to doing it.

• After reading about the different life losses that can impact your current loss, write down which ones you have already experienced. How do you feel they have impacted your ability to mourn your current loss? Have you identified something that could improve your ability to do so? Write it down and commit to doing it.

• What lessons did you learn from your relationship that gave you perspective or way of looking at things? Take time and write down each lesson, what you learned, and why you find it valuable.

• What mindset will you need to support making life changes? Will this mindset be new for you? Please write what you think it will take for you to make such changes and adopt a new mindset. Consider who can support your plan to change. Pick a trusted friend and share this with them.

• If you are at a place where you can begin to look to the future with hope, what would be your theme song as you move into this new life? Is there another song you considered but didn't choose? What about that song made you eliminate it?

• Write about the life you'd like to have moving forward. Write about what you would like to be a typical day in your life. It's challenging to make a plan unless you know where you are going. Make your plan as detailed as you can. Remember, it's just a plan; you can always change it.

• Do you sense an increased openness to allow grief to wash over and through you? What helps you cope while you grieve?

• What behaviors did your loved one engage in that you admired or enjoyed the most? Write these down and note how your life was made better by these acts.

- Thinking of all the gifts you received from your loved one, which one(s) do you want to pass on within your family or perhaps your community or the world?  Pick one or two and make a plan for how you will pass them on.

- Where are you in terms of finding meaning in your loss?  If you have found meaning, what is it and how does this impact your grief?

- Where are you now in terms of re-engaging with life again? If a year has passed and you are avoiding social situations, or not enjoying former hobbies, for example, what is standing in your way?  Write down everything that comes to mind without screening your thoughts. Pick a roadblock that you would be open to working on and think of small steps you could take to overcome it and what support you will need to do so.  Write down your intention to take this step.

- What are your fondest memories of your loved one?

- What are the funniest memories you recall? Does laughter hurt or help right now?

- I'll always remember when you would say, "_____." This inspired me because_____

- The happiest times I remember were _____.

- The most difficult times we went through were _____. From this I learned _____.

# ONLINE RESOURCES

Please note that these online sites were up and working at the time of publication.

**Accidental Impacts**
Coping with inadvertently causing a deadly accident.
https://accidentalimpacts.org

**Actively Moving Forward (AMF)**
Connects and supports young adults ages 18-30 including college students to actively move forward in honor of their person. Includes a free app to connect and provide resources to members.
https://healgrief.org/actively-moving-forward/

**Alive Alone**

For bereaved parents whose only or, all children are deceased. https://www.alivealone.org

**Bereaved Parents of the USA**

Provides support to bereaved parents, siblings and grandparents.
https://www.bereavedparentsusa.org

**Compassionate Friends**

Offers support for family after the death of a child. https://www.compassionatefriends.org

**First Candle**

Providing support for grieving families who have lost a child to SIDS.
https://firstcandle.org/online-support-groups/

**Friends for Survival**  Providing peer support services for those grieving the suicide of family or friends. https://friendsforsurvival.org.

**Grief Anonymous Facebook Online**

Offering over 20 grief-specific confidential Online grief groups for those with Facebook accounts.
https://griefanonymous.com/facebook-groups/

**Grief in Common**
Offers a live chat room to connect with others.
https://www.griefincommon.com/pages/about/

**Grief Healing**
Providing professionally monitored and moderated online message boards for all kinds of losses.
https://www.griefhealingdiscussiongroups.com/

**GriefNet.org**
Offers support to bereaved parents, siblings, and Grandparents. https://www.griefnet.org

**National Alliance for Children's Grief**
NACG raises awareness about the needs of children and teens who are grieving a death, providing education and resources for anyone who supports them. https://childrengrieve.org/

**Online Grief Support**
Connect with others grieving a similar loss.
https://www.onlinegriefsupport.com/groups

**Open to Hope**
Finding hope after loss. https://www.opentohope.com

### The Forgiveness Project

Collects and shares stories from both victims, survivors and perpetrators of crime and conflict who have rebuilt their lives following hurt and trauma. https://www.theforgivenessproject.com

### The Rainbow Bridge

Provides support for those grieving the loss of a pet of any kind. https://www.rainbowsbridge.com

### Tragedy Assistance Program for Survivors (TAPS)

Provides comfort, care, and resources to those grieving the death of a military loved one. https://www.taps.org/

### World Without Hate

Mission: Breaking the cycle of hate and violence through empathy, education, and storytelling.. https://worldwithouthate.org

# ONLINE ETHICAL WILLS

An ethical will is a document written to communicate values, wisdom, history, stories, and love from one generation to another.

### Life Legacies

"Preserving Past and Present for the Future." The website offers templates for ethical wills as well as tips on how to write one. It also showcases writings of interest to those who want to prepare to write their own ethical will. https://life-legacies.com/index.html

### Thinking Beyond the Numbers

Offers suggestions for an Ethical Will, including templates and worksheets to get started. https://www.thinking beyondnumbers.com/what-is-an-ethical-will/

# END NOTES

1. National Vital Statistics Mortality Data
htpps://www.cdc./nchs/nbss/deaths.htm

2. Excerpted from Shadowlands: A Play, William
Nicholson, Plume–Penguin Books USA,, New York
City, NY, 1991. Used with permission of the author.

3. Excerpted from The Grief Recovery Handbook, 20th
Anniversary Expanded Edition, John W. James,
Russell Friedman, Harper Collins Books, New York, NY,
2009, (pg.)56. Used with permission of Russell
Friedman, author.

4. Norton, Michael, I., and Francesca Gino. "Rituals Alleviate Grieving for Loved Ones, Lovers and Lotteries." Journal of Experimental Psychology: General (forthcoming) https://nrs.harvard.edu/urn3: HUL.InstRepos:10683152

5. American Heart Association. Is Broken Heart Syndrome real? https:/www.heart.org> what-is-cardiomyopathy-in-adults

6. Excerpted from We Bereaved, Hellen Keller 1929, Leslie Fulenwider, Inc, New York, NY. (p) 2.

7. Excerpted from Man's Search for Meaning, Viktor Frankl, Washington Square Press, Boston, MA, 1984, (p)135. Used with the permission of the publisher.

8. Nada Psychic tears and the Science of Crying." The Swaddle, March1, 2019. https://theswaddle.com/ psychic-tears-and-the-science-of-crying.

9. WBUR: 20 Years After a White Supremacist Almost Killed Him, He's Dedicated His Life to Changing Hearts. https:// wbur.org/kindworld/2019/11/26/ change-of-heart.

10. Excerpted from Out of Solitude: Three Meditations on the Christian Life, Henri Nouwen, 2004, Ave Maria Press Notre Dame, IN, (pg.) 38. Used with permission of the publisher.

# ABOUT THE AUTOR

Marsha Barnosky's social work career spans 45 years, with over 20 years in hospice and palliative care. Local counselors frequently called, searching for resources for grieving clients. Realizing that seasoned counselors felt uncomfortable working with those grieving a death inspired her to open her psychotherapy practice for those facing grief, loss, and trauma. A Michigan native, Marsha received her Bachelor's degree from Western Michigan University, and her MSW from Wayne State University. When not writing, she enjoys painting, time with family and friends, and "haunting" cemeteries, appreciating the history, architecture, and serenity of the surroundings. She lives in Fruitport, Michigan near the Lake Michigan shore with her husband Carl and their feisty Cavachon, Oscar.

Made in the USA
Monee, IL
02 September 2022

11967134R00098